Praise for *Discerning Your Call to Ministry*

Discerning Your Call to Ministry offers us a path forward to cut through the popular subjectivity and confusion often surrounding the term "calling" in order to provide thoughtful and scripturally informed guidance for those exploring steps toward ministry and ministry preparation. Readers will find each chapter to be a source of wise help and helpful wisdom, enabling them to think carefully, reflectively, and deeply about truly important questions regarding church, ministry, and service. I trust that Jason Allen's fine book will receive the wide readership it deserves.

DAVID S. DOCKERY
President, Trinity International University

Everyone headed toward vocational ministry should take the time to read *Discerning Your Call to Ministry*. Each believer has a calling from God to be on mission for Him, no matter where He has placed us, but the call to ministry brings with it important questions, self-study, and considerations. My friend Jason Allen has put together a helpful roadmap that will bring greater clarity and focus to your ministry calling. It is an investment you will be grateful you made.

KEVIN EZELL
President, North American Mission Board, Southern Baptist Convention

Navigating through your call to ministry is a spiritual journey. One of theological education's brightest stars, Jason Allen, provides profound but also practical insights to helping you through your journey of discerning God's call in your life. Answering the questions raised in this book will lead you to a life and ministry of faithfulness to God and the calling He has placed upon your life.

RONNIE FLOYD
Senior Pastor, Cross Church
Immediate Past President, Southern Baptist Convention

I believe in a God-called ministry. Not a ministry that is achieved, but one received from the Lord (Colossians 4:17). For this reason, I am so glad my good friend Jason Allen has written *Discerning Your Call to Ministry*. This book is encouraging and engaging and invites us to know and do the will of God. Every person who desires to respond to God's call for ministry should read this book.

JACK GRAHAM
Pastor, Prestonwood Baptist Church

For years I've wrestled with these very questions posed by Jason Allen. I trust you'll find his guidance as helpful as I did. If you're a prospective pastor, pick up this book and talk it over with a mentor. If you're a current pastor, keep some copies handy and pray God raises up future ministers in your midst.

COLLIN HANSEN
Editorial Director, The Gospel Coalition
Author of *A God-Sized Vision: Revival Stories that Stretch and Stir*

A man's calling into gospel ministry is of paramount importance and should be taken with the greatest seriousness. *Discerning Your Call to Ministry* asks the hard and necessary questions as you seek God's direction and call upon your life. This book is for those who are dealing with the question of God's call and for those who have been convinced of that call for many years. This is the book you have been looking for as you seek to fulfill your calling for God's glory.

STEVEN J. LAWSON
President, OnePassion Ministries, Dallas, TX

God's call to full-time ministry is a concept few people understand or explain well. It's not a mystical form of special revelation or an audible voice from heaven. And God doesn't call men to pastoral ministry without gifting them for the task and sovereignly drawing their hearts to the work. (Which suggests there are a lot of people doing pastoral ministry today who were never called to the task.) Jason Allen skillfully outlines and explains the vital biblical principles for discerning whether a person is truly called to ministry. This helpful handbook answers scores of questions I hear from young men and potential seminary students all the time. I'm grateful for the help this volume will be and the influence I know it will have.

JOHN MACARTHUR
Pastor-Teacher, Grace Community Church, Sun Valley, CA

One of the hardest questions I faced as a teenager was this one: how do I know if the call I feel to ministry is genuine? I wish I had had this book. Jason Allen is an experienced, thoughtful guide on what it means to serve Christ's church as pastors and teachers. This book will not only help young would-be ministers to discern their calling, but will also equip pastors and church leaders to disciple the next generation. The church has needed this book for a long time.

RUSSELL MOORE
President, Ethics & Religious Liberty Commission, Southern Baptist Convention

This is a courageous and bold book dealing with one of today's most neglected subjects in the church. I am grateful to our Lord that Jason Allen has taken up the task to write this much-needed book. This is precisely what we need in the church today. To my knowledge there is no other guide that is as clear and straightforward on discerning one's call to gospel ministry as this one. It is thoroughly and gloriously biblical from beginning to end, and I heartily commend it.

BURK PARSONS
Copastor, Saint Andrew's Chapel, Sanford, FL
Editor, *Tabletalk* Magazine

Not every day does one hear the wisdom of the ages from one of the youngest seminary presidents in America. *Discerning Your Call to Ministry* is a crisp, phenomenally perceptive introduction to the ministry that ought to be read by every young man considering the ministry. Steeped in insights from the Scriptures and from Charles Haddon Spurgeon, Allen adroitly weaves his way through every salient query that needs to be the focus of a prospective preacher. I am especially thankful for Allen's emphasis on the essential call of God to the ministry and for the importance of the pastor's home. Headed for the ministry? Drop by this book on your way.

PAIGE PATTERSON
Southwestern Baptist Theological Seminary, Fort Worth, TX

How do I know if I'm called to ministry? How do I know if I'm ready to serve in ministry? These are two of the common questions I am asked again and again. Now I have the perfect response: read Jason Allen's *Discerning Your Call to Ministry*. This book is thoroughly biblical. It is immensely practical. And it is incredibly helpful. It is now my number one recommendation to those who sense God's call to ministry in their own lives.

THOM S. RAINER
President and CEO of LifeWay
Author of *Who Moved My Pulpit?*

Gospel ministry is no light thing, and Jason Allen asks the right questions—probing, challenging, revelatory—in an eminently pastoral way to help those seeking the Lord's will on the matter. *Discerning Your Call to Ministry* is a reliable guide to the gravity and gladness of the vocation of Christian ministry from a wise and experienced leader.

JARED C. WILSON
Managing Editor of For The Church (ftc.co) and author of *The Pastor's Justification*

JASON K. ALLEN

DISCERNING YOUR CALL TO MINISTRY

HOW TO KNOW FOR SURE AND WHAT TO DO ABOUT IT

MOODY PUBLISHERS
CHICAGO

All Scripture quotations, unless otherwise indicated, are taken from the New American Standard Bible®, Copyright © 1960, 1962, 1963, 1968, 1971, 1972, 1973, 1975, 1977, 1995 by The Lockman Foundation. Used by permission. (www.Lockman.org)

Scripture quotations marked ESV are from The Holy Bible, English Standard Version®(ESV®), copyright © 2001 by Crossway, a publishing ministry of Good News Publishers. Used by permission. All rights reserved.

Edited by Matthew Boffey
Interior and Cover design by Erik M. Peterson
Cover illustrations by Dave Wright

All websites and phone numbers listed herein are accurate at the time of publication but may change in the future or cease to exist. The listing of website references and resources does not imply publisher endorsement of the site's entire contents. Groups and organizations are listed for informational purposes, and listing does not imply publisher endorsement of their activities.

Portions of this book are adapted from articles previously posted online.

Library of Congress Cataloging-in-Publication Data

Names: Allen, Jason K., author.
Title: Discerning your call to ministry : how to know for sure and what to do about it / Jason K. Allen.
Description: Chicago : Moody Publishers, 2016.
Identifiers: LCCN 2016028402 | ISBN 9780802414663
Subjects: LCSH: Christian leadership. | Christian leadership—Biblical teaching. | Vocation—Christianity.
Classification: LCC BV652.1 .A45 2016 | DDC 253/.2—dc23 LC record available at https://lccn.loc.gov/2016028402

ISBN: 978-0-8024-1466-3

We hope you enjoy this book from Moody Publishers. Our goal is to provide high-quality, thought-provoking books and products that connect truth to your real needs and challenges. For more information on other books and products written and produced from a biblical perspective, go to www.moodypublishers.com or write to:

Moody Publishers
820 N. LaSalle Boulevard
Chicago, IL 60610

3 5 7 9 10 8 6 4 2

Printed in the United States of America

To my loving wife, Karen.

Since before we wed, when I first sensed God's
call to the ministry, you have been wholly devoted
to me and the ministry He has entrusted to us.
"My Husband, My Ministry" is more than
a class you teach, it is a life you live.
Without you my life and ministry would
be infinitely lacking. With you I am the
recipient of ten thousand joys.

Totus tuus.

CONTENTS

Foreword   11

PREFACE:
Sharing My Journey and Understanding Yours   13

INTRODUCTION:
What Does It Mean to Be Called to Ministry?   17

1. *Do You Desire the Ministry?*   25
2. *Does Your Character Meet God's Expectations?*   33
3. *Is Your Household in Order?*   49
4. *Has God Gifted You to Preach and Teach His Word?*   61
5. *Does Your Church Affirm Your Calling?*   73
6. *Do You Love the People of God?*   83
7. *Are You Passionate about the Gospel and the
   Great Commission?*   93
8. *Are You Engaged in Fruitful Ministry?*   103
9. *Are You Ready to Defend the Faith?*   113
10. *Are You Willing to Surrender?*   123

CONCLUSION:
So Are You Called?   131

APPENDIX:
Advice for Seminary   141

Notes   149
Acknowledgments   153

FOREWORD

Winston Churchill once tried to explain Russia by describing the vast nation as "a riddle wrapped in a mystery inside an enigma." Throughout history, many others have shared Churchill's frustration.

For too many Christians, a call to ministry seems just as puzzling. How does a young man know that God has called him to ministry?

Some evangelical Christians, otherwise clear-headed about doctrine and the Christian life, reveal a deep confusion over the call to ministry—descending into mysticism or reducing the call of ministry to nothing more than a subjective experience.

At the same time, the Christian ministry is not a mere profession and a call to preach is not something that can be simplified into a checklist used by guidance counselors.

The Bible reveals both the glory and the burden of the call

to ministry, and what we need is a faithful and pastoral presentation of the biblical vision of that call. Thankfully, that is just what Jason Allen provides in this book. He combines biblical wisdom with a very practical vision of the call to preach.

He clears away the confusion and faithfully sets out what the Bible reveals about what we rightly call the gospel ministry. He knows what is at stake. In every generation the church needs a new corps of preachers and leaders, ministers, and missionaries. Our Lord taught us to pray for workers for the harvest, and so we must.

When I was a young man, evangelical churches habitually talked about the task of "calling out the called." I don't hear that talk so much now, and I think it is because churches are themselves confused about how God actually calls the minister.

I believe that God will use this book to help "call out the called." It is timely and timeless in its approach, and it will be especially helpful to those considering a call to the ministry. *Discerning Your Call to Ministry* will also help the church in the task of calling out the called. That will be a great gift to all Christians.

R. Albert Mohler, Jr.
President, The Southern Baptist Theological Seminary, Louisville, KY

PREFACE

SHARING MY JOURNEY
AND UNDERSTANDING YOURS

I well remember the swirling emotions that filled my heart as I processed God's call to ministry. Though I grew up in a Bible-believing, Southern Baptist church, I resisted the gospel throughout my childhood and adolescent years. It was not until my freshman year in college that I committed my life to Christ. After many months convicting my heart, the Holy Spirit invaded my life, saved me, and redirected my life's ambitions.

Yet, for me, God's call went beyond His summons to salvation. Over the next three years I increasingly sensed His call to ministry as well. Looking back now, it seems so clear, so inevitable, and so right. Then, however, it was much more confusing, even daunting. Spiritually I felt as though I was navigating my way through a maze, incrementally gaining clarity and direction, but unsure of what would be my final destination.

I spent some two years in suspended animation, feeling called to ministry but unsure how that was supposed to feel. I desired the ministry, but I wondered if that was an appropriate desire. I felt at once wholly unworthy of the call, yet disobedient if I did not pursue it. I heard the testimonies of others who had surrendered to ministry and I could identify with them, but only in part. From a distance, the whole process looked imperceptibly mystical.

Further complicating matters, I had watched others publicly declare their intent to pursue ministry, yet never follow through. Every time this occurred I felt in some small way that God's reputation was sullied. I did not want to jump the gun and add my name to the list of those ministers who failed to launch.

Moreover, certain questions kept haunting me:

- How could I know for sure this was not just a temporary zeal for Christ?
- What if my passion was only a phase of life—like many experience during their college years—that would wane with age and other responsibilities?
- Might God simply be calling me to be a committed layperson?
- How, exactly, does God issue His call?

- Would surrendering to ministry mean a life of sacrifice and hardship?
- If I spurned God's call, was I inviting His punishment?

Wanting answers, I searched the Scriptures and sought wise counsel. I daily devoured the Pastoral Epistles and intuitively sought out opportunities to minister. I taught Sunday school, led evangelistic outreach, became a summer youth intern, ministered in prisons, preached in halfway houses, and went on an overseas mission trip, sensing that if God were indeed calling me, I would increasingly desire the work.

My desire to do other things withered, and my desire to serve Christ flourished. My appetite for ministry became insatiable. The more I preached, the more I longed to preach. The more I served, the more I desired to serve. The more I witnessed, the more I wanted to be Christ's witness.

Ultimately, Paul's airtight argument on the necessity of gospel preaching sealed it for me: "How then will they call on Him in whom they have not believed? And how are they to believe in Him of whom they have never heard? And how are they to hear without a preacher? And how will they preach unless they are sent? Just as it is written, 'How beautiful are the feet of those who bring the good news!'" (Rom. 10:14–15).

If my deliberative process had been a set of scales weighing divine confirmation, it was as though God placed his finger on the side of ministry, pushing the balance down with over-whelming, irrefutable consent. Fear gave way to confidence, answers displaced questions, and doubt was replaced by assurance. God was indeed calling me to the ministry.

Now, nearly two decades later, I find myself on the other end of these queries and conversations. As a seminary president, I regularly visit with those wrestling with a call to ministry—and they are experiencing questions and feelings I know all too well.

Like I did many years ago, most Christians have an undeveloped, insufficiently informed understanding of what it means to be called to the ministry. They are often in their own state of suspended animation, seeking certainty and assurance yet feeling ill-equipped to follow God's call.

These are urgent and consequential deliberations. After all, what could be more unsettling than to embark on the ministry unsure if God is indeed leading you? Even the best of ministries can be challenging enough, but to undertake ministry without a clear sense of God's call, accompanied by God's power and God's favor, is too much to bear.

At the same time, God's call is too noble, too consequential, and too glorious to neglect. You need to know for sure whether or not God has called you. And you can.

INTRODUCTION

WHAT DOES IT MEAN
TO BE CALLED TO MINISTRY?

"I think God is calling me to ministry." This is how a conversation began years ago when I was a pastor. A young man, Mike, had come to me for help discerning his call to ministry. I thanked Mike for reaching out to me, and then probed further. "Tell me, what is God doing in your life? In what way do you sense God's call?"

Mike went on to share how his faith was growing, how he was increasingly eager to share the gospel, and how he wanted to be a better witness for Christ. I was pleased to hear of Mike's heart for evangelism, and as I listened I encouraged him in this.

But I stopped short of affirming a call.

Why is that? Because what Mike was describing wasn't in and of itself ministry; it was Christianity—how every believer is to live. It is wonderful, of course, but there are aspects of the ministry that go beyond what every Christian is called to do.

My conversation with Mike is representative of many I've had over the years, and it reveals that the phrase "called to ministry" is often robed in confusion. Regrettably, many well-intentioned individuals have announced a call to ministry, and many well-intentioned churches have affirmed them, without truly knowing what they mean. You don't want to be part of their number, and I suspect that's why you're reading this book. So let's clarify what we mean when we say "called to ministry."

CALLED . . .

We should begin by noting that calling, generally speaking, isn't reserved for Christian ministry. In fact, this is one of the helpful clarifications from the Protestant Reformation. The Roman Catholic Church fostered a class distinction between clergy and laity that placed ministerial work on a higher plane. It was understood to be more noble, meritorious, and therefore favored by God and men. In a very real sense, laypersons were considered second-class citizens. Secular work was "earthly," something you settle for if you are not set apart for ministry. Even the sacramental system, which made laity dependent upon the clergy for communion with God, supported this distinction.

Martin Luther and the other Reformers reasserted the biblical concept of *vocation*, which holds that God calls and gifts every person for an occupation. Calling is not limited to the ministry; it reaches into every arena of life. In God's kind providence He orders not only His church, but also society, gifting persons for service in each.

To be sure, there is a distinction between the clergy and laity, but the distinction concerns calling, gifting, and biblical qualification, not worth, nobility, or access to God. The farmer, banker, educator, and physician are all created in God's image, gifted and called by Him to serve the church and community, and they can do so with God's favor and with deep, internal fulfillment. Every Christian should pursue their occupation as a vocation—a calling by God—and should seek to fulfill it in a way that brings Him glory.

So are you called? Yes! But now let's consider what it means to be called to the ministry. We'll distinguish this from two other categories: called to minister and called to ministry.

Called to minister

Every Christian is *called to minister*. As I explained to Mike, to minister—or to serve the body of Christ—isn't for a select few. It is part and parcel of the Christian life. The

New Testament makes this clear in multiple passages. First Corinthians 12–14 and Romans 12 show how God gifts every believer to function in the body of Christ. As each believer fulfills his or her God-assigned role, the church is strengthened and the believer increases in fruitfulness. In Ephesians 4, Paul explains that pastors, ministers, and evangelists are given for the equipping of the saints *for the work of the ministry*. All saints—regardless of their vocation—are to be active in building up the body of Christ.

Called to ministry

The second category we might think of is *called to ministry*. By this I mean that your vocation has a direct ministerial component to it. You do not have to meet 1 Timothy 3 qualifications or be ordained, but you have consciously chosen to walk through a door of ministerial service—for example, as a children's ministry coordinator, teacher at a Christian school, or Christian camp counselor.

In my own seminary context, many of our faculty and senior staff were at one time ordained to the ministry but now serve God by training pastors, ministers, and missionaries. Additionally, we have other employees like accountants, IT staff, and administrative assistants, who have followed God's call out of the secular workforce to serve here in a ministerial capacity, often taking significant pay cuts. The extent to which the latter group is "in ministry" depends on their particular context, role, and even personal intent. If they are serving as unto the Lord, have undertaken their position with a sense of calling, are actually engaged in serving the church through the seminary, and are consciously sacrificing to help train pastors and ministers for the church, they may well think of that work as ministerial. On the other hand, if they were just seeking a paycheck and the position struck them as a good career opportunity, or it has no direct connection to serving the church, then not so much.

Called to the ministry

The third category for consideration is *called to the ministry*. This is the final formal category, defined in the New Testament in places like Ephesians 4:11–16, 1 Timothy 3:1–7, and Titus 1:6–9.

In Ephesians 4:11–12, Paul says, "And He [Christ] gave some as apostles, and some as prophets, and some as evangelists, and some as pastors and teachers, for the equipping of the saints for the work of service, to the building up of the body of Christ . . . " In the main, the church has long understood the offices of apostle and prophet as reserved for the first century, ceasing to exist with the death of the apostles and the completion of the New Testament. Here we will consider only the offices of pastor, evangelist, and teacher.

Whatever their distinctions, these offices all share one common charge: minister the Word. The same charge falls upon overseers. This is why, in 1 Timothy 3:1–7, Paul lists only one skill—"able to teach"—alongside the many character qualities an overseer must have. In the next chapter I will discuss why a pastor is essentially an overseer, but my main concern here is to establish what a call to the ministry essentially *is*: a call to the ministry of the Word. Stated another way, a call to preach or teach the Word is the distinguishing mark of a call to the ministry.

This is not to suggest that only those with a formal preaching position are truly called to the ministry, but that those called to the ministry are called first to teach or preach the Word, and should undertake their ministry accordingly. The ministry of the Word can show up in many different venues and express itself in many different formats, including worship leadership, counseling sessions, college ministries, classroom lectures, and the like.

Whether you are called to minister, called to ministry, or called to the ministry, your service matters. Every Christian has a holy duty to do his or her work as unto the Lord, and the following pages can help you render your service honorably. That said, this book focuses on the third category, and its goal to help you discern that call.

For me, discerning God's call was a road I had to travel, an exploratory journey that ultimately led to a place of assurance. Then I desperately wished for a road map; now I want to give you one. What follows are ten questions, biblically framed, to help you search your life and discern your call. My hope is to waive off those not called and reassure and encourage those who are—to lead you toward clarity, one way or the other.

As you begin this book, take comfort in knowing that if you are called to the ministry, you have been called by God—and if not, it's because He has called you to something else.

Clearly, this is the biblical pattern—God calls, God commissions. As John Newton, the infamous slave trader who became a gospel minister and penned the immortal hymn "Amazing Grace," observed, "None but he who made the world can make a minister of the gospel."[1] It is indeed a holy summons; ministers are set apart by a holy God for a holy work.

Pause and reflect on these passages (emphases mine):

- "The harvest is plentiful, but the workers are few. There-fore beseech *the Lord of the harvest to send out workers* into His harvest" (Matt. 9:38).
- "The Holy Spirit said, '*Set apart for Me Barnabas and Saul for the work to which I have called them*'" (Acts 13:2).
- "Be on guard for yourselves and for all the flock, *among which the Holy Spirit has made you overseers*, to shepherd

the church of God . . ." (Acts 20:28).

- "How will they preach *unless they are sent* . . . "
  (Rom. 10:15).

- "*He gave some* as apostles, and some as prophets, and
  some as evangelists, and some as pastors, and teachers . . . "
  (Eph. 4:11).

God's call begins internally, described as "God's voice heard
by faith."[2] Perhaps it is that internal voice, that internal yearning, which has prompted you to pick up this book. That's a
good sign. Read on.

This internal call occurs in different ways in different people.
Don't be concerned if you haven't known a Damascus Road–
like experience. Some do, but most don't. As Oswald Chambers
said, "The realization of a call in a person's life may come like a
clap of thunder or it may dawn gradually. But however quickly
or slowly this awareness comes, it is always accompanied with
an undercurrent of the supernatural."[3]

Anyone can choose the ministry, and many people have.
Such individuals may draw a paycheck from a church or religious entity, but they are not necessarily serving God. Only
a select few—divinely set apart and summoned by God—are
truly ministers of the gospel.

Has God set you apart? Might He be calling you? Read on
and find out.

QUESTION #1

DO YOU DESIRE
THE MINISTRY?

M artyn Lloyd-Jones was one of the greatest preachers of the twentieth century. He pastored the Westminster Chapel in the heart of London for nearly three decades, and by the end of his ministry he was one of the most influential ministers on earth. But before Lloyd-Jones was a great preacher, he was an accomplished physician. After earning his medical degree, he came under the tutelage of Lord Horder, caregiver to His Majesty, King George V, and enjoyed one of the most promising medical careers in all of England.

In considering God's call to ministry, Lloyd-Jones wrestled

with his "physician's dilemma"—giving up medicine to pursue preaching. Ultimately, it was a war of desire, and his desire for ministry won out: "We spend most of our time rendering people fit to go back to their sin! I want to heal souls. If a man has a diseased body and his soul is all right, he is all right to the end; but a man with a healthy body and a distressed soul is all right for sixty years or so and then he has to face eternity in Hell."[1]

Lloyd-Jones well understood how God channeled the minister's desires toward confirmation of calling. He reflected:

> I would say that the only man who is called to preach is the man who cannot do anything else, in the sense that he is not satisfied with anything else. This call to preach is so put upon him, and such pressure comes to bear upon him that he says, "I can do nothing else, I must preach."[2]

If ever a young man resonated with Lloyd-Jones' description it was me, circa 1997. I felt an unprovoked, unintended desire for ministry, and I did not know what to do with it. That desire—and whether or not it was even appropriate—dominated my life. I did not know where to turn or what to do, but, thankfully, God drew me to the Pastoral Epistles.

First Timothy, 2 Timothy, and Titus are often called the Pastoral Epistles because they reflect most directly on pastoral service. In them Paul sets forth how the church is to minister and who should lead that ministry. When I was discerning my call, I read through these letters daily to better grasp what a life of ministry entails, how one is to serve the church, and, especially, to clarify God's will for my life. They were like road signs and streetlights, both pointing and illuminating the way forward.

The most helpful passage in the letters for anyone sensing God's call to the ministry is 1 Timothy 3:1–7, as it states plainly the qualifications for the ministry. From verse one I derive our first question: *Do you desire the ministry?*

APPROACHING THE PASTORATE

In 3:1 Paul writes, "It is a trustworthy statement: if any man aspires to the office of overseer, it is a fine work he desires to do." This singular verse is pregnant with meaning and is key to discerning your call to ministry. Let's unpack it piece by piece.

It is a trustworthy statement. On five occasions in the Pastoral Epistles Paul says, "It is a trustworthy statement." Each time, he does it to draw particular attention to a word or phrase of special importance. Here, he uses it to introduce the qualifications for ministry, reminding us that they are essential for both the church and the would-be minister. In other words, we should sit up and pay careful attention to what follows!

Aspires. This is an uncommon New Testament word. It means "to reach out after" or "grasp for." We can think of this as the practical act of seeking the office of overseer. Common expressions of this in our day are applying for a ministry position, seeking mentorship from a pastor or elder, enrolling in seminary, or entering a ministry training program.

Office of overseer. This is the subject of verses 1–7, and it refers to both a title and task, or form and function. By form and function I mean the correspondence between what someone is called and what they do. Those who are pastors in title (form) must do what pastors, biblically defined, do (function). Conversely, if a person is not qualified to exercise authority in the church (function), you don't get around it by downgrading their title to "minister" or "director" (form). They are still positioned to exercise authority in the church, thus functioning as a pastor or elder. The term *overseer* refers to one who exercises spiritual leadership over a congregation. As we will see, this office also carries with it pastoral care responsibilities, a duty to preach or teach Scripture, and a requirement to meet certain character qualifications. Scripture also says that those who labor well in it are worth double honor—that is, full-time elders (pastors) should be supported financially by their church (1 Tim. 5:17).

Depending on your Bible translation, *overseer* may also be translated "bishop." In the New Testament, *overseer*, *bishop*, *elder*, and *pastor* are used interchangeably. For example, here in 1 Timothy 3:1 the word *overseer* is the Greek word *episkopos,* which is sometimes translated "bishop," and from which the Episcopal Church gets its name. It is synonymous with the Greek word *presbyteros*, meaning "elder," and from which the Presbyterian Church gets its name. We see these terms, and the word *pastor* (Greek *poimen*), used interchangeably in places like Acts 20:17–38, 1 Peter 5:1–2, and Titus 1:5–7. The same scenario occurs in 1 Timothy 5:17 when Paul calls the overseers "elders." Therefore, in this book we will use *pastor, elder, bishop,* and *overseer* interchangeably, and in so doing we will anchor their qualifications and functions to 1 Timothy 3:1–7.

Fine. The work of ministry is a fine work. *Fine* means "noble," "honorable," or "excellent." This means that yearning for ministry is a good thing. Be encouraged, if you find yourself aspiring to the ministry, that the work is not only worthwhile but exceedingly glorious, and it is worthy of your full effort and pursuit.

Desire. This word refers to the inward compulsion, or passion, for ministry. It is what's taking place in your inner person that leads you to "aspire," or pursue practically, ministerial service. These two words—*aspire* and *desire*—must go together. If you desire the ministry, you will aspire to it.

To do. With this phrase Paul puts the minister's task on an active, energetic footing. Again, the wording is subtle but important. The office of the pastor is not merely a position to be occupied; it is a work to be done. For a number of years I had the privilege of pastoring near Fort Knox, Kentucky. Nearly half of my church was military, and I enjoyed spending many days on base. One day while eating lunch with a group of soldiers, I noticed that officers wore their ranks on their shoulders, whereas the enlisted soldiers' chevrons were positioned on their arms. When I asked about it, I learned that the placement of an officer's rank on his shoulder signified the burden of leadership he carried. Conversely, the enlisted soldier's rank on the arms indicates the brawny nature of his work, serving his country with strength and arms.

We should think of the pastoral office similarly, except that a pastor wears his ranks on both his shoulders and his arms. There is no such thing as a pastor who knows only the burden of leadership or only the sweat of service. He who desires the ministry must aspire to both, since the ministry necessarily includes both. A pastor serves the people of God and carries out his responsibilities as assigned by Scripture and God's people.

EAGER TO SURRENDER

First Timothy 3:1 brought refreshing and liberating clarity to my "desire dilemma." Though I desired the ministry, I was conflicted as to whether I *should* desire it. I feared I was being presumptuous, perhaps even arrogant. My confusion was rooted in the phrase "surrendering to ministry." The phrase was common in my home church, and it prompted me to assume one should resist ministry until ultimately relenting and surrendering to it. As we'll see in chapter 12, ministry does require surrender, but not necessarily the type preceded by resisting God's call.

In 1 Peter 5:1–3, the apostle underscores the appropriateness, and even the necessity, of desiring the ministry. Peter writes:

> Therefore I exhort the elders among you, as your fellow elder and witness of the sufferings of Christ, and a partaker also of the glory that is to be revealed, shepherd the flock of God among you, exercising oversight not under compulsion, but voluntarily, according to the will of God; and not for sordid gain, *but with eagerness;* not yet as lording it over those allotted to your charge, but proving to be examples to the flock. (emphasis added)

A simple reading of the passage shows us that pastors must desire the ministry. There is no other way to shepherd God's flock but with eagerness. Alexander Strauch, in his book *Biblical Eldership*, agrees:

> The desire to be an elder is not sinful or self-promoting, if it is generated by God's Spirit. . . . A Spirit-given desire

for pastoral leadership will naturally demonstrate itself in action. It cannot be held in. A man who desires to be a shepherd elder will let others know of his desire.[3]

Every Sunday might not furnish the preacher with emotions like Richard Baxter, who famously resolved to preach "as a dying man, to dying men; as one not sure to ever preach again."[4] But the one whom God is calling will have a growing desire for the work of ministry.

If you're contemplating ministry, desiring the work isn't just an appropriate feeling; it is an indispensable one. As Charles Spurgeon said, "The first sign of the heavenly calling is an intense, all-absorbing desire for the work. In order to be a true call to the ministry there must be an irresistible, overwhelming craving and raging thirst for telling to others what God has done to our own souls."[5]

Do you desire to serve in ministry? If you do, your desire is not the final step—it's the first, and your stamina in pursuing each subsequent step will reveal the intensity of your desire. Next we turn to perhaps the most scrutinizing question in this journey of discernment: *Does your character meet God's expectations?*

DOES YOUR CHARACTER MEET GOD'S EXPECTATIONS?

As a seminary president, I receive lots of mail. Publications from every sector of life flood my office daily, and I enjoy perusing many of them, especially those related to theological education. I am often amused and sometimes even frightened by much of what I read, as these publications demonstrate that much of what passes for theological education is shockingly unbiblical.

A couple of years ago, one such magazine caught my attention. It was the institutional magazine for one of America's more progressive seminaries. Institutional magazines like this are typically little more than puff pieces meant to celebrate the institution's achievements and update the school's constituency on campus happenings and positive developments.

Against this backdrop, the magazine's featured story stopped me in my tracks. The article, "Extending the Gift of Welcome to All," highlighted a student's homosexual lifestyle and ministry pursuit. The student was an alternative-lifestyle advocate who engaged regularly in homosexual activity.

My interest intensified as I read of the student's perceived call to ministry and ensuing pursuit of theological education. He reflected on his interaction with the seminary administration and community, noting, "I didn't go there [to the seminary] looking for them to say, 'You're gay and I affirm you.' I wanted to go there and hear, 'You're in ministry, and I affirm that,' and I felt that from day one."[1]

Embedded within that statement is ruinous logic. At first glance, one might find the dichotomy between one's lifestyle and call to ministry acceptable—even appealing—especially in the modern milieu of subjective, autonomous spirituality. However, a closer look at the New Testament reminds us that the Bible does not afford us this option. To be called to ministry, one must possess a lifestyle that passes scriptural muster. God's Holy Spirit, who calls, does not contradict God's Holy Word, which confirms.

QUALIFICATIONS FOR MINISTRY

First Timothy 3:1–7 (and, similarly, Titus 1:6–9) make clear that God's standard for ministry is high. The threshold is high because the office is high. The office is high because we serve a high God who zealously guards the glory of His name and church. If you do not meet God's standard for the ministry, you can be sure He isn't calling you to it.

The passage offers a clear and nonnegotiable list of character qualifications for gospel ministry. The qualifications are prescriptive, not descriptive—that is, they didn't only apply in Timothy's day (descriptive); they apply today, too (prescriptive). To be sure, in ministry it might be helpful to be winsome and eloquent. It seldom hurts to possess a magnetic personality. Yet these external traits mean nothing if you don't meet the qualifications of 1 Timothy 3. Furthermore, the qualifications do not represent a one-time threshold to cross. Rather, they mark a lifestyle to be maintained, character to be cultivated, and ongoing accountability to God's Word and God's people. One's call to ministry is inextricably linked to one's godly character. The two cannot—and must not—be decoupled.

Over the next three chapters, we'll consider each qualification with the care and intentionality the ministry deserves. Before us is not a pileup of words, it is God's divine standard for ministry service.

It is a trustworthy statement: if any man aspires to the office of overseer, it is a fine work he desires to do. An overseer, then, must be above reproach, the husband of one wife, temperate, prudent, respectable, hospitable, able to teach, not addicted to wine or pugnacious, but gentle, peaceable, free from the love of money. He must be one who manages his own household well, keeping his children under control with all dignity (but if a man does not know how to manage his own household, how will he take care of the church of God?), and not a new convert, so that he will not become conceited and fall into the condemnation incurred by the devil. And he must have a good reputation with those outside the church, so that he will not fall into reproach and the snare of the devil.

1 TIMOTHY 3:1–7

NOT JUST ANY MAN WILL DO

Overseers are men

We've already discussed verse 1, except for one important word: *he*. Throughout 1 Timothy 3:1–7 and every biblical text that references the office or work of an elder the candidate is referred to as a man. A simple reading of this passage makes plain that God intended the primary leadership role within the church to be reserved for men only.

This male headship is not due to first-century cultural prejudices. Rather, as the previous chapter makes clear, it is rooted in God's created order (1 Tim. 2:9–15; cf. Gen. 2:22). God intended complementarity between the genders, both within the home and the church. While both men and women are endowed with equal worth and dignity before God, in His unsearchable wisdom He established the office of pastor/elder for qualified men only.

Women are still gifted to serve the church in many different and important ways. We should encourage and celebrate such service. For instance, at Midwestern Baptist Theological Seminary we happily admit women into our programs of study. We invest in them as servants of Christ, and those called by God to minister and maybe even to ministry. As we do, we make clear our convictions that the office and function of the pastor/elder are biblically reserved for qualified men.[2] So if you are a woman reading this book, please read on. God has indeed called you to minister, and He may even be calling you to ministry, and I hope that this book will strengthen you for both of these callings.

Though the office of pastor/elder is only open to men, not just any man will do. Let us continue to examine the text to see what is required of him.

Above reproach

This passage is bookended by two catchall phrases that summarize God's standard for ministry. The first phrase, *above reproach*, means "to be blameless, above accusation." It doesn't mean "perfect," and if it did, churches would be without ministers. Rather, it pertains to one's reputation. When people think of you, do they think of you as having a minister-like character? Additionally, one must be blameless before the onlooking world, so that he will not "fall into reproach and the snare of the devil" (v. 7). These two bookending phrases form the perennial standard required of those who desire the ministry. Living "above reproach" is the foundation of all the other qualifications.

We gather from this that to live above reproach requires wisdom and discernment. For example, I once knew a minister who had a heart for ministering to prostitutes. His burden was noble and right, but he had to use extreme caution in ministering to these women. Though his intention was pure, if he had been caught alone with a prostitute his ministry would have been ruined.

Such is the sting of "above reproach" and "of good reputation." Whether it's your fault, someone else's fault, or no one's fault, a lack of discretion can put you in a compromising situation, thus marking you as unfit for ministry. As Peter reminds us, the pastor's life must be worthy of emulation, for he is to be an example to the flock of God (1 Peter 5:3).

CHARACTER ABOVE REPROACH

Within these general "above reproach" expectations, we now get a more specific, detailed listing of God's requirements. If "above reproach" and "good reputation" deal with outward appearance and standing, these next qualifications deal more with the inward, the heart.

Self-disciplined

For the sake of succinctness, and due to their similarity, we can combine "temperate," "prudent," and "respectable" under one heading—*self-discipline*. These three form a triad of personal restraint and self-direction.

To be *temperate* is to be level-headed and sober-minded. An overseer cannot be erratic, impulsive, or easily influenced by whims and wishes, whether his or another's. This obviously includes refraining from substance abuse of any kind, since this would alter the pastor's mind and impair his judgment, but it goes beyond that to include his general consistency of mind. The reason for this qualification is clear: a pastor makes many important decisions in fulfilling his office, and he must be capable of sound judgment.

Prudence refers to a person's ability to lead himself, which is essential for leading others. A prudent person is disciplined and prioritizes well. He doesn't endlessly surf the web, scan social media, or binge on Netflix while life's responsibilities pile up. The orderliness of his life earns the esteem of others, and it reveals his fitness to order rightly the local church. Prudence is especially needed when you consider the age in which we minister. We've managed to extend adolescence into a lifestyle; young and old alike don't value discipline and restraint but rather overindulge on leisure and entertainment. The qualified minister is prudent, mature, and balanced.

Respectable ups the ante, taking prudence to the structural, formal level. A respectable man has his affairs in order. He can expend himself for the ministry because he has rightly planned, prepared, and ordered his life. Self-discipline is a hallmark of a respectable life, thus the minister disciplines himself "for the purpose of godliness" (1 Tim. 4:7). Is your life sufficiently structured to enable ministry, or will your life pattern impair it? Is your life marked by drama and chaos or maturity and faithfulness? The concern is both testimonial and practical. Is your life marked by a Christian, ministerial decorum? The point is not mild-manneredness, but a life not prone to impetuousness. Practically, such maturity, stability, and self-discipline is necessary for optimal ministry service.

Not addicted to wine

Though the Bible never forbids the drinking of alcohol per se, it does warn about the downfall of excessive drink, the sin of drunkenness, and alcohol's many other pitfalls. In the first century, drinking wine and wine mixed with water was done for reasons of sanitation. That's why Paul encouraged Timothy to drink a little wine for his stomach.

On this point, John MacArthur brilliantly captures the importance of a minister's self-discipline, writing, "If a man cannot control his life when he is alone, he does not belong in the pastorate. If he is the kind of person who needs to have a committee to keep him in line, he will end up bringing grief to the church."[3]

Since becoming a Christian, I've practiced total abstinence. Now, as one who leads a seminary, I encourage those in ministry to do the same. I acknowledge that the Bible never explicitly forbids consuming alcohol; my argument is one from prudence. Considering the many liabilities and social pathologies associated with alcoholic excess and intoxication, and in light of our "above reproach" expectation, I think it is wise to abstain. Many churches expect this of their ministers, and complying will help you remain above reproach in their eyes.

Free from the love of money

Being "free from the love of money" is a recurring concern in Scripture, and it is as relevant today as it was when Paul penned these words two thousand years ago. Read the news consistently for a week and you will see that money is a magnet able to pull anyone into darkness. To be free from the love of money is to be outside of its magnetic field, safe from its allure.

Practically speaking, this qualification has a healthy, pruning effect. The truth of the matter is that most every person in ministry makes less than they would in secular work. Churches don't typically attempt to pay ministers a secular market rate for a comparable profession—nor should they—and this helps keep men who love money out of the pulpit.

On a deeper, attitudinal level, if money is a driving ambition, it will cloud your judgment and compromise your ability to discern ministry opportunities. In other words, if you "follow the money," you'll likely follow it right out of the ministry—and perhaps even into ruin.

Hear Paul's wise warning to us: "Godliness is actually a means of great gain when accompanied by contentment . . . Those who want to get rich fall into temptation and a snare . . . For the love of money is a root of all sorts of evil, and some by longing for it have wandered away from the faith and pierced themselves with many griefs" (1 Tim. 6:9–10). For the pastor, there is no such thing as being too free from the love of money.

Assuredly, but not recently, converted

Paul insists that the one set apart for ministry must not be a new convert. Though we are not given a clear time threshold, we gather one must be a certain and maturing Christian.

You cannot rightly show others the way of salvation if you have not walked it yourself; you cannot point people to eternal life if you will one day know eternal death. Nothing in the entire world is more tragic—or more ruinous to a church—than an unconverted minister. This is why Paul puts an overseer's conversion to the test of time. Time always proves the authenticity of one's faith. As weeks turn into months, the fruit of one's conversion will make plain one is in the faith.

This requirement is unique in that Paul states the danger of ignoring it: falling into the snare of the devil. When churches bring up ministers without sufficient time for maturation, they harm the minister and potentially damage the church. Unfortunately, I have witnessed this scenario on more than one occasion. One man I know was pushed forward too quickly for ministry. He bombed his interview with the ordination council and was embarrassed before the congregation and his family. The tragedy is he was a great guy with good intentions. Good intentions are important, but they aren't enough. Spiritual maturity and biblical formation—which cannot be microwaved—must be present in the one pursuing ministry.

INTERPERSONAL QUALITIES

The heart-evaluation that 1 Timothy 3:1–7 presents us with is most closely associated with our character—who we are in our inner person, and the reputation that character has earned us. But Paul also touches on how our interactions with other believers prove our fitness for pastoral leadership.

Hospitable

Hospitable means "to love strangers" or "be willing to welcome and serve those in need." It points to a disposition of warmth, concern, and openness to all, especially to Christians. To be a faithful pastor, you don't have to be an extrovert, but you do have to be hospitable. An extrovert is a personality type (which, admittedly, can be helpful in ministry), but hospitality is a choice. You choose to welcome, love, and serve those who are under your care.

This is a biblical expectation, but it will also help your ministry practically. Hospitality provides venues for the shepherd to be with his sheep and get to know them in more intimate settings. It communicates care, concern, and vulnerability, which build trust. In moments of crisis, grief, or rebuke, you will be glad that you filled the relational bank through hospitality.

Rest assured, you and your spouse don't need to be Martha Stewarts to pull this off. The simple acts of opening your home, sharing meals, introducing yourselves, engaging in conversation, and inquiring about your guests' lives and needs are all marks of hospitality. Biblical hospitality is so rare in our day that even the smallest gestures will go a long way.

Amicable

With this word I join three dispositions mentioned in verse 4: not pugnacious, gentle, and peaceable. To be pugnacious is to be abrasive or combative, physical or otherwise. *Pugnacious* means "to strike" or "to attack." The minister doesn't settle disputes with his fists, nor does he fan the flames of strife. On the contrary, he reacts calmly and kindly. More than a few ministers have lost their reputations by blowing their gaskets in tense moments. I know one pastor who got into a fistfight during a church softball game. That regrettable scene ended his ministry right then and there. The shepherd who loves his sheep doesn't have a pattern of exploding when he engages them.

Gentle stands in stark contrast to belligerence. To be gentle means to be "genial, forbearing, and gracious." It doesn't require weakness or passivity, and it doesn't preclude one from standing strong or even being confrontational when the occasion demands, like in critical matters of Christian belief and practice. It means you view God's children like your own; you are forgiving and forbearing, seeking their highest good.

Peaceable is similar to gentle, and means "reluctant to quarrel." Divisiveness plagues many churches, and that division often starts at the top. The faithful pastor strives to "preserve the unity of the Spirit in the bond of peace" (Eph. 4:3). He understands that Satan revels in a church fuss and loves to taint the body of Christ. We must seek the Pauline balance of "truth and love." There are issues worth debating that could legitmately split a church, but the pastor who loves the church understands that dissension is to be avoided and a church split is a last resort.

LEADERSHIP,
A TRICKLE-DOWN PHENOMENON

Why does God place such an emphasis on the moral purity of his servants? Because God's glory is on display in His church. Every pastor is a steward of God's glory, and every pastor influences his church, for better or worse. In this way the local church is like any other organization: those who lead it will dramatically impact it. If a pastor is godly, prayerful, and vibrantly following Jesus, over time his church will reflect those virtues. The stakes are indeed high. Paul reminded Timothy that the church is "the pillar and support of the truth" (1 Tim. 3:15). So goes the leadership, so goes the church. Nothing less than the preservation and proclamation of the truth is at stake.

If a pastor is carnal and shallow, over time the church will likely reflect his shortcomings as well. Sadly, I've seen this phenomenon on a number of occasions. It is nearly impossible for a church to rise above its spiritual leadership, especially if those leaders have been well entrenched for any length of time. A. W. Tozer said it well, "The minister must experience what he would teach or he will find himself in the impossible position of trying to drive sheep. For this reason he should seek to cultivate his own heart before he attempts to preach to the hearts of others."[4] Put simply, a pastor can't lead his church spiritually where he has not been.

You don't need to be perfect to be a minister, but you do have to be above reproach. When God calls a man to ministry, he also qualifies him—that is, He tests a man according to His own Word. If you think you are called to ministry, but you don't meet God's standards, then you are mistaken. Don't run through flashing yellow lights. Pause, seek counsel with your pastor, and make sure God is indeed leading you down the road of ministry.

As the apostle Paul closes, "Pay close attention to your self and to your teaching; persevere in these things, for as you do this you will ensure salvation for yourself and those who hear you" (1 Tim. 4:16). There is much at stake when a man shepherds a flock of God. This is why God guards the position with a high wall of requirements. We continue scaling this wall in the next chapter.

QUESTION #3

IS YOUR
HOUSEHOLD IN ORDER?

Having five young children ensures life is never boring. What comes out of their mouths, especially in public settings, is often unforeseen, uninvited, and unforgettable. Like many families, we have one child who is especially prone to such embarrassing locutions. He's a free thinker, quick-witted, incapable of forgetting what his parents wish he would, and always on standby, ready to spout out that one comment or story that brings maximum embarrassment.

On one occasion a few years ago, a family in our church had invited him over to play with their children. After an afternoon of playtime, my wife stopped by to pick him up. As Karen surveyed the strewed room, she suggested our son help their kids pick up the toys, knowing he likely helped make the mess.

In front of their entire family—parents included—our son blurted out, "Oh mom, their house was already a mess when I got here. In fact, it's a wreck every time I come over. We don't have to clean it up. This is how they like it!" In that moment, my wife was horrified, incalculably embarrassed, probably wishing she was dead. Such is life with young children.

That anecdote reminds me of the priority the apostle Paul places on the minister's family. For those pursuing ministry, all of our life—not just moments of comical outbursts—projects a story, a testimony to our fitness for ministry. As ministers our premier concern is not off-the-cuff comments by a rambunctious child, but the steady, consistent testimony of our families.

First Timothy 3:1–7, in addition to making clear that your calling cannot be separated from your character, makes clear that it cannot be separated from your family. An evaluation of your fitness for ministry must include an evaluation of your household.

A ONE-WOMAN MAN

Verse 2 says an overseer must be the "husband of one wife." Obviously, this phrase precludes polygamy, homosexuality, and adultery, but it does not preclude unmarried men from serving in ministry. After all, the apostle Paul himself was single. It means that you must be the husband of *only* one wife, not that you must have a wife.

Husband of one wife is smoothed out from the literal translation, "a one-woman man." Paul is saying the qualified man is given only to one woman. This certainly includes the bounds of matrimony, but it goes well beyond it. He is married to one, and only one, woman; he loves one, and only one, woman; and he physically and emotionally knows one, and only one, woman.

To be sure, the gospel minister fights daily with the impulses of temptation. He knows the lust of the flesh well, and, given Satan's desire to imperil his ministry, he probably knows it too well. Yet he works to guard his eyes, cultivate a clean heart, and channel his affection exclusively to his wife.

While lust is as old as the fallen man himself, the twenty-first century presents particular challenges associated with it. Pornography is rampant in our society, and temptations abound. Those who regularly digest pornography are unfit for ministry. If you find yourself struggling to some degree with pornography, you should discuss this with your pastor and others who are helping you discern your call to ministry. The nature, frequency, and timing of your struggle are all factors, but if viewing pornography is a current pattern of your life, then it has compromised your fitness for ministry.

As it relates to divorce, many honorable, evangelical Bible scholars disagree over precisely what "a one-woman man" stipulates. Specifically, if you were once divorced, are you permanently disqualified from ministry? What if your divorce occurred prior to your conversion? What if, due to your former wife's infidelity, your divorce was on biblical grounds?

Given the totality of 1 Timothy 3:1–7, including the "above reproach," "husband of one wife," and "well-ordered household" qualifications, my default position is that one who has been divorced is most likely unfit to serve as a pastor. That doesn't mean he can't fruitfully serve the church in other capacities, but I believe 1 Timothy 3 seems to bar him from pastoral service.

Admittedly, this is a knotty issue with many potential nuances and caveats, making it impossible to fully unpack it in a book like this. If you are divorced and believe God is calling you into ministry, I'd encourage you to seek out your pastor or elders, invite them into your life to evaluate your circumstances, and seek their counsel and affirmation for the best way forward.

The main point, ultimately, is that an overseer must maintain fidelity to his wife. This reminds me of Billy Graham's famous "Modesto Manifesto."

No name in the twentieth century was more associated

with gospel ministry than Billy Graham's. Graham was a titanic figure, ubiquitous in American life for over a half-century. He preached the gospel to millions, was the confidant to tenUS presidents, and was the face of American evangelicalism. Though Graham's political associations, evangelistic methodologies, and ministerial ecumenism drew criticism, he remained a cultural and ecclesiastical icon.

For having a public ministry that spanned seven decades, he was remarkably scandal-free. Televangelists fell into sex scandals, and prosperity preachers into financial ones, but Graham proved above reproach. He erred on the moral safe side, and as a young man he pledged himself to the Modesto Manifesto.

Meeting in a hotel room in Modesto, California, in 1948, Graham and his associates drafted a covenant to minister with utmost integrity. The Modesto Manifesto stipulated ministry convictions, financial integrity, and marital fidelity. As to the last, it stated that Graham would never be alone with a woman other than his wife. Graham knew you might not have an affair if you are alone with a woman; but if you are not alone with a woman, then you cannot have an affair (or be accused of having one).

Graham's high road gave no foothold for the devil, and it helped ensure he would maintain faithfulness to his wife and enjoy a fruitful ministry. We would be wise to follow his example.

A WELL-ORDERED FAMILY

Whether we like it or not, the pastor is not an autonomous agent, hired by the church without consideration of his family status. If a church is willing to do that, they merely want a church mascot, not someone to fulfill the full calling of pastoral ministry. The New Testament picture of the pastor is much more inclusive and robust.

In verse 4, Paul insists that a pastor "must be one who manages his own household well, keeping his children under control with all dignity." He then adds this word of explanation in verse 5, "If a man does not know how to manage his own household, how will he take care of the church of God?"

Within evangelical circles there are differing views on the full meaning and scope of the household qualification. Does this mean that pastors are responsible for the sins of their adult children, who no longer live at home? If the expectation is for every child to be converted, by what age must they follow Christ?

We must take care not to speculate on the passage's meaning and instead respect the plain sense of it. Its purpose is not to place an expectation on our children, but to place an expectation on our leadership of them. The household should reflect a biblical pattern and be flavored with the presence of Christ. The wife should be a believer, endorsing and supporting her husband's ministry. The children themselves should clearly reflect Christian-parental oversight, not given over to rebellion and thus damaging the minister's witness.

While the pastor cannot microwave conversion or obedience in the hearts of his children, he must faithfully nurture them in the fear and admonition of the Lord. The point is not for the church to search for blemishes in our children. The point is that your family's orderliness is a reflection of your leadership. One child out of four going wayward probably reflects more on the child than on your ability to disciple and lead. Three children out of four going wayward may reflect more on your leadership.

Admittedly, there is a level of subjectivity to this qualifying point. If you are in ministry, you should be in conversation with your lay leaders to help you interpret this qualification in light of your particular family's season and the expectations of the church. If you are contemplating ministry, and your family is in such disarray as to be an obvious liability to your ministry, then you most likely should not be pastoring.

Balance and wisdom are essential. We don't want our ministry pursuit to become a weighty expectation for our family where they are more actors than people, living in a legalistic bubble of religious decorum. The point is that a well-ordered family reflects our ability to lead, disciple, and manage a church. Be honest with yourself: are you taking proper care of your household? (And if you aren't married, are you taking care of yourself?)

PROTECTING YOUR FAMILY

I want to digress here, briefly, from the qualification for ministry to an expectation of ministry: your family's involvement in the church.

A few years ago, while interviewing a potential staff member for a church ministry position, I was struck anew by the sensitivity of the matter. The interview was going smoothly until a committee member inquired about the role the candidate's wife would play in his ministry. The young man became defensive, insisting the church was hiring him, not his wife. That brief exchange nearly torpedoed his candidacy, and it left me puzzled.

In the previous months, I had gotten to know the couple personally. He was a great guy, and his wife seemed to fully support him. In fact, in many ways I viewed them as a model couple, well balancing ministry and family. That is why I was surprised by the young man's response.

After further conversation, I discovered that it wasn't that the couple was reticent to give themselves to the church—both were eager to serve—but that the man had been coached by others in ministry to protect his wife. It was an appropriate concern inappropriately expressed. That scenario was indicative of a long-standing question for pastors and churches alike —how do we rightly balance ministry and family expectations?

This tension is felt by all who serve the church. It resides just under the surface in many congregations. Sadly, many men leave the ministry due to erring one way or the other in what is often a delicate balance.

In the mid-twentieth century—during the heyday of programmatic and event-driven ministry—churches prioritized pastoral presence. In many churches the pastor was expected to be virtually omnipresent. The dutiful parson was always roaming hospitals, making house calls, and presiding over every church function. In addition to limiting his time for sermon preparation, it often compromised his ability to lead his family.

In its most excessive forms, congregations expected their pastors to lead ever-growing ministries, even at the expense of their families. I know of one pastor who said, "A man has to choose. He can have either a great family or a great ministry. He cannot have both." Other more budget-minded churches expected a "buy one, get one free" scenario. If you hire a man to pastor, then surely his wife will play the piano, coordinate the nursery, or direct the children's ministry for free, right?

The pendulum clearly needed to swing the other way, and thankfully in most contexts it has. Yet at times I fear the pendulum has swung back too far. We must protect our families, but we need not sequester them. Balance is hard to find, but it must be sought.

Many of my fondest family memories have been in the context of ministry, and many of my fondest ministry memories have occurred with my family present. Often I've made hospital visits, home visits, or shared the gospel with a child or two by my side. Over the years, my kids have heard me preach hundreds of sermons, sat through scores of seminary chapel services, and participated in dozens of church outreach projects. We've sought to make such outings enjoyable so that they made the body of Christ more attractive to our kids, not less.

If we really believe in the glory of the church, and of the splendor of God's call to ministry, then it is not something from which we shield our families. We should expose them to it. I have learned that, oftentimes, choosing between family and ministry is a false choice. Why not just bring the family along?

That said, there are of course times when you ought to especially guard your family's time. The wise man is always observing, always learning more about his wife and children. Different life stages, particular ministry contexts, and the personality of the minister's wife all influence their participation. If your season of life is particularly challenging, just be up-front and state plainly your needs to the church. Most likely they will understand.

Over the years, my wife has been a wonder woman, resolutely supportive of my ministry. Yet, there have been seasons —like when our five kids were ages five and under—that required unique energy and attention at home. That required me, and my places of service, to understand.

One last comment: don't be discouraged if the first time you raised the subject of your ministry calling with your wife, she had misgivings. The Bible calls us to lead and love our wives in an understanding way. Fear of the unknown might prompt initial reluctance. Pray for her and with her, share your heart, and include her as you seek wise counsel. The good news is, if God is calling you, He will call her, too.

We must remember that ministry in the New Testament is life-on-life. For Paul, the church was not a distant group before which he occasionally appeared. They were his spiritual family, with whom he lived and ministered. This means that even if you could get a ministry position, without a qualified or supportive family you should let it pass. You'd immediately be stymied in your ministry, the church would be hindered, and your family would be put in an impossible situation. It's better to first take care of priority number one, your family. After you have rightly ministered to them, and they are led and nurtured, then you can pursue ministering to the church.

Is God calling you to the ministry? If He is, it isn't in spite of your family, but along with them. Is your household in order? Is your wife supportive of your call? These are vital questions that must be addressed as you determine your calling to ministry. After you've addressed them, then you can consider other questions, like whether you're gifted for the ministry. To this we now turn.

QUESTION #4

HAS GOD GIFTED YOU TO PREACH AND TEACH HIS WORD?

In the midst of the 2008 global financial crisis, Warren Buffet famously observed, "Only when the tide goes out do you discover who's been swimming naked." Buffet was reflecting on the banks and financial firms that had insufficient capital to meet their financial obligations during the steep market downturn, but his words apply to the ministry as well. Preaching and teaching God's Word has a way of stripping ministers bare; it exposes us and puts our gifting on public display. You can't finesse your way through preaching with polished appearance, warm people skills, or seminary credentials alone. When you stand before God's people with Bible in hand, the tide goes out. It is in those moments of truth, when you attempt to speak on behalf of God, that all will see the veracity of your calling.

ABLE TO TEACH

The Greek phrase translated "able to teach" occurs in the New Testament only in 1 Timothy 3:2 and 2 Timothy 2:24. It simply means "able to explain God's Word with skill." The emphasis is not so much on the knowledge of Scripture, though that is included, but on the ability to communicate it effectively. Teaching may take the form of preaching, but it can take other forms as well. Not all called to the ministry will preach, but all must be able to teach God's Word. The rest of this chapter will focus primarily on preaching, which I define simply as "teaching with passion." Both preaching and teaching convey biblical truth, but preaching includes public proclamation—heralding the truth of Scripture to the gathered congregation. It is a difference of venues or outlets. As a wise brother once told me, preaching should never be anything less than teaching the Bible, but it should always be more than a Bible study.

It is interesting that the ability to teach is the only qualification listed that has to do with a person's gifting or ability. The would-be pastor doesn't have to be a skilled negotiator, competent manager, or creative genius. He doesn't need a charismatic personality, certain IQ, or impressive academic pedigree. There is one gift, and only one gift, a pastor must possess. He must be able to teach.

Though "able to teach" is the only qualification related to gifting, it is a stiff one. Throughout Scripture we see the gravity of being God's spokesman. James warns us, "Let not many of you become teachers, my brethren, knowing that as such we will incur a stricter judgment" (James 3:1). And the author of Hebrews tells us, "Obey your leaders and submit to them, for they keep watch over your souls as those who will give an account" (Heb. 13:17). We dare not take up this task without a sense of gravity, seriousness, and consequence.

Since the pastor's primary duty is to preach and teach God's Word (Eph. 4:11–12), he who would hold the office must be equal to the task. Literally, lives are at stake. "Keep a close watch on yourself and on the teaching," Paul says to Timothy. "Persist in this, for by so doing you will save both yourself and your hearers" (1 Tim. 4:16 ESV). The health of the church rises or falls with the pulpit because it's God's Word that builds up a church (Eph. 4:11–14). The pastor's task is a weighty, consequential one.

WHY PREACHING?

Preaching is God's divinely ordained means of communicating His Word, nourishing His church, and redeeming a people for

Himself. Other ministerial activities may complement preaching, but no ministerial activity should displace it. Preaching is a theme that runs across the whole Bible, consistently described and prescribed throughout both Testaments. No passage sets forth the charge quite like 2 Timothy 4:2, "Preach the word; be ready in season and out of season; reprove, rebuke, exhort, with great patience and instruction."

This charge is situated at the end of Paul's final letter to his son in the faith, Timothy, and it encapsulates the broader biblical expectation that ministers persist in their duty to faithfully preach and teach the Word. The twelve apostles also defended the primacy of preaching, as demonstrated in Acts 6. When a complaint arose among the Hellenist believers that their widows were being neglected, the twelve gathered all the disciples together and ordered this solution:

> It is not right that we should give up preaching the word of God to serve tables. Therefore, brothers, pick out from among you seven men of good repute, full of the Spirit and of wisdom, whom we will appoint to this duty. But we will devote ourselves to prayer and to the ministry of the word. (Acts 6:2–4 ESV)

The apostles knew their priorities, and preaching the gospel was at the top of the list. Charles Spurgeon, "The Prince of

Preachers," held the same convictions:

> I do not look for any other means of converting men beyond the simple preaching of the gospel and the opening of men's ears to hear it. The moment the church of God shall despise the pulpit, God will despise her. It has been through the ministry that the Lord has always been pleased to revive and bless his churches.[1]

God only had one Son, and He made Him a preacher. Scripture tells us, "Jesus came preaching," and then He sent His disciples out to preach (Mark 1:14; Matt. 28:16–20). From the prophets of old to Pentecost, and even to the end of the age, preaching is God's appointed means. This is why we preach.

WHAT DO I PREACH?

As Paul penned 2 Timothy, he knew his own death was near. Christians were being persecuted. False prophets were plaguing the church. Many who once professed Christ as Savior had since fallen away. Timothy himself was vacillating in the faith and questioning his call. In this setting, Paul wrote his final letter, the dying words of a dying man, to a distressed church and a discouraged son.

In chapter 3, Paul documents the catastrophic effects of

man's sinfulness. He mentions lust, envy, greed, arrogance, treachery, and more, and then he presents their ministerial antidote to these ailments: the preaching of God's Word. This is a striking connection. In light of the darkness of the times, the growing band of false teachers, and the onslaught of persecution—three realities that confront every generation of ministers—Paul calls Timothy to preach the Word. This charge sprouts from the bedrock of Scripture. It comes not only after documenting the challenges ministers will face, but also after one of the grandest testimonies to Holy Scripture in all the Bible: "All Scripture is inspired by God and profitable for teaching, for reproof, for correction, for training in righteousness; so that the man of God may be adequate, equipped for every good work" (2 Tim. 3:16–17). Preaching is necessary and powerful because of the inspiration, truthfulness, authority, sufficiency, and effectiveness of Holy Scripture. We are called to preach the Word because the days are evil and the Scriptures are powerful. The Bible is our sure and unfailing word from God. And as we preach it, it is the guarantor of our sermon.

For preachers, 2 Timothy 4:2—"Preach the word"—has a certain romance to it, a magnetic pull calling us back again and again and again to our central responsibility. The straightforward call to preach—in light of so many problems in the society and the church—appears simplistic, but those are God's instructions, and the longer I live, the more I see how wise they are. When the days are evil and faith is weak, when persecution rises and hope grows faint, only one Word can strengthen, and only one Word can save: God's.

If you are not convinced of Scripture—its truthfulness, authority, relevance, and power—then you will be disinclined to preach the Word, and you will preach your own word. You may look to the Bible for sermon points because that is what evangelical preachers are to do, but you'll never let the Word be the point and substance of your sermon, and so your sermons will lack true power.

The Bible is our message. It is a perennial word. It is a necessary word. It is more than a resource book. We don't look to it occasionally to diagnose problems, like doctors trying to decide what medicine to prescribe. Rather, we preach from it in and out of season, knowing it will expose the sickness in our hearts while also healing us by the Word of Christ. That is why, each week, those who are called to preach are called to preach the Word.

Even in our architecture, church buildings convey the centrality of preaching. The Protestant Reformers moved the pulpit from the side of the sanctuary to the front and center. This move demonstrated that the preaching of the Word of God, not the celebration of the Eucharist, was most central to worship.

Additionally, the Regulative Principle—which clarifies the essential elements of true worship—argues that where the

Word has not been preached, the saints have not worshiped. The congregation may have enjoyed a concert or participated in a warm fellowship, but corporate worship does not occur apart from corporate proclamation.

HOW DO I PREACH?

God has not only predetermined what we preach, but also how we preach. We know this both descriptively and prescriptively. Descriptively, we see biblical sermons, like those in the book of Acts, as explanations of the Old Testament text, and this gives us a model for how to preach from both the Old and New Testaments. Prescriptively, as we just reviewed, we are commanded to "preach the *Word*." God never tells us to tout our own wisdom—only His. This is why we should aim to preach in a way that most optimally brings God's Word to bear on the lives of the congregation.

Because God wants His *whole* word proclaimed, expository sermons—sermons that explain a passage along its own contours, place it within its broader biblical context, and bring it to bear on God's people—are preferred. The best way to accomplish this is to move through entire books of the Bible, one literary unit at a time.

There is a measure of latitude here. Whether the sermon is thirty minutes long or sixty, or if the sermon series is counted in weeks or years, we can find joy when God's Word is honored, explained, and authoritatively preached.

While wit, a booming voice, and strong presentation skills are helpful, the key ingredients of a faithful preaching ministry are the study and proclamation of the Word, and you should strive to cultivate both. To emphasize either to the de-emphasis of the other is error. Here we must maintain intentional balance.

Some more naturally enjoy the process of preparing sermons. They enjoy digging into the text of Scripture, rightly interpreting it, constructing an exegetical outline and stitching together a sermon. This is good, and no one should enter ministry without regularly delving into the text. Others more naturally enjoy the presentation. The act of preaching itself animates them. They enjoy delivering the goods to God's people, as well they should. However, great preachers excel at both, and faithful preachers work to strengthen both their study of the Word and the resulting proclamation.

MEASURING YOUR ABILITY

Like any other ability, teaching and preaching God's Word is an acquired skill. Gifted by the Spirit of God, yes. But practice makes perfect, and it might take quite some time to clarify your gifting to preach.

I remember the first time I preached. The event took place

in a halfway house for women suffering from abuse. On Sunday afternoons, I occasionally accompanied a friend, who usually did the preaching. On one occasion, he invited me to go and asked me to handle the preaching responsibilities.

Throughout the week I spent my spare time crafting the sermon—if one can call it that! I jotted down my favorite Bible verses, pulled together all the preacher jargon I had ever heard, and wrote out my personal testimony. When the moment of truth came, I preached to the best of my ability. I thought I had thirty minutes' worth of "stuff," but made it through my notes in less than half that time. On the fly, I just returned to the top of my notes and went through them once more to fill the time.

At the conclusion of the sermon, I gave an invitation and several women came forward for prayer. I left on cloud nine, feeling God's pleasure. On the ride home, my friend said to me, "It made you feel good when those ladies came forward, didn't it?" I shot back, "Incredible. It was incredible." My friend smiled and said, "I know the feeling. Those same ladies come forward every week."

In hindsight, that sermon was an absolute train wreck. Even now, I pray that sermon wasn't recorded and doesn't show up in my life someday. My feeble attempt to preach was earnest, but the finished product was no doubt laughable.

I share my story with you as encouragement. Don't expect to sound like a veteran preacher your first time in the pulpit.

In fact, you may not ever become an accomplished preacher. Rather, seek your godly counselors, pastors and elders, to affirm your gifting. The key is, more people than your mother ought to benefit from your preaching and perceive your gifting.

Martyn Lloyd-Jones famously observed that preaching is "the highest, the greatest, and the most glorious calling to which one can ever be called."[2] In fact, it is too high and too glorious of a calling for just anyone to preach just anything for just any reason in just any way.

Do you share this fervor for faithful proclamation? Does the preparation and delivery of sermons fulfill you? Do the people of God benefit from your ministry of the Word? Does your church sense a gifting in you and affirm your ability to preach or teach? If yes, these are signs you have the gift of teaching.

Preparation, practice, and godly mentorship can mature the preacher. Seminaries can grant a degree and churches can hire a pastor. But only God can make a preacher. Do not pursue the ministry if God has not gifted you to teach. One of the best ways to know if He has is to receive input from your community of faith. As you will see in the next chapter, woe to anyone who pursues the ministry apart from his church's blessing.

QUESTION #5

DOES YOUR CHURCH AFFIRM YOUR CALLING?

A few years ago, while living in Louisville, I was invited to join one of Kentucky's most exclusive clubs. Located downtown, the Pendennis Club is one of the state's most historic and prestigious societies. Its membership included Senator Mitch McConnell and other leading Louisvillians.

Friends who were members had invited me to lunch there a few times over the years. The dining room was a sight to behold. Century-old hardwood floors, ornate trim work, antique furniture, old-world sconces, and historic art all adorned the room. The dining hall—and the entire building—felt like a throwback to yesteryear, a twenty-first-century, Americanized Downton Abbey.

I quickly sensed that membership wasn't for me. Given all that membership entailed, financial and otherwise, I wasn't interested in joining. But one part of the membership process intrigued me. To be a member of the Pendennis Club, you had to be nominated by a current member in good standing, cosponsored by several others, and affirmed by the entire membership.

In other words, you didn't seek membership; membership sought you. You didn't call them; they called you. You didn't apply; you were nominated. For your nomination to be successful, other members in good standing had to vouch for you, and the whole club had to affirm you.

The call to pastoral ministry is similar. You don't select the church; the church selects you. In the New Testament there are no rogue agents or self-appointed ministers. Every legitimate pastor has a church standing behind him. Church affirmation is essential to the call to ministry.

THE CHURCH'S AFFIRMATION

As we've seen in this book, your call to ministry includes an internal desire for the office and external character alignment with 1 Timothy 3:1–7. In both cases, the local church is positioned to assess and validate your fitness for ministry.

We see hints of this in Paul's letters to Timothy. Writing to his beleaguered son in the faith, Paul instructs, encourages, and assures Timothy by reminding him of the community's affirmation:

- "Do not neglect the spiritual gift within you, which was bestowed on you through prophetic utterance with the laying on of hands by the presbytery" (1 Tim. 4:14).
- "For I am mindful of the sincere faith within you, which first dwelt in your grandmother Lois and your mother Eunice, and I am sure that it is in you as well. For this reason I remind you to kindle afresh the gift of God which is in you through the laying on of my hands" (2 Tim. 1:5–6).

In addition to these charges to Timothy himself, Paul also instructs Timothy in affirming the gifts of others:

- "The things which you have heard from me in the presence of many witnesses, entrust these to faithful men who will be able to teach others also" (2 Tim. 2:2).
- "Do not lay hands upon anyone too hastily and thereby share responsibility for the sins of others; keep yourself free from sin" (1 Tim. 5:22).

When you consider these examples, as well as the councils that surrounded important appointments of leaders—like Judas's replacement in Acts 1 and the deacons in Acts 6—a clear pattern emerges: the church appoints its own leaders. Leaders do not appoint themselves.

This is in line with the nature of the call. Since pastors are undershepherds of God, not just anyone can take up the post. God, in His wisdom, has made the church a natural vetting instrument. While this vetting authority might be channeled procedurally through a ministry team, elder board, or other group acting on behalf of the church, that doesn't negate the congregation's role in affirming one's gifts and recommending him for ministry.

This process also ensures that a would-be minister earn his reputation through faithful and consistent service. Ideally, no church would affirm a call to ministry without having seen enduring signs of that call. And furthermore, because of the plurality inherent in a congregation, this process guards against oversight or favoritism. If a host of saints agree on one's fitness for ministry—can affirm his character and teaching ability—chances are the man is indeed qualified.

As you can see, the church is responsible for commissioning pastors to the ministry. It would be unwise, if not disobedient, to bypass community affirmation in pursuing the call.

THE HOLY SPIRIT'S AFFIRMATION

If God is calling you to ministry, it won't just be a matter between you and your church. The Holy Spirit will be working simultaneously in you, your pastor, and ultimately the entire congregation. This is a part of God's kind providence over your life and the entire "call to ministry" process. If He is calling you, the desire He has placed for ministry within you will be paralleled by a desire on the part of others—your pastor and your church—for you to do ministry. Your call to ministry will become increasingly evident to all.

I love how Martyn Lloyd-Jones describes the Holy Spirit's work in your life and the church simultaneously, jointly, leading both toward confirmation:

These are the ways in which the Church tests a man who says that he has received a call. My contention is that God works through the man himself and through the voice of the Church. It is the same Spirit operating in both, and when there is agreement and consensus of opinion you are right in assuming that is a call from God.

A man does not appoint himself; he is not put into the ministry merely by the pressure of the Church. The two things go together. Both sides have been neglected. I have known many cases where men have been pushed into the ministry, who were never meant to be there, by false teaching on the part of the Church. The two things must go together.[1]

On a practical level, the way to discern if the Holy Spirit is working in you and your church to affirm your calling is simple: talk to your church. Specifically, seek out your pastor and/or the other elders. If you serve in a larger church where getting an appointment may take some time, seek out a church staff member or other lay leaders.

Though it will vary from church to church, the process will probably begin like my previously mentioned conversation with Mike. The conversation will be informal. You will simply share what you perceive God is doing in your life. Your pastor most likely will be kind and supportive, and he will ask questions to help you clarify God's will.

Ideally, the conversation will not come as a surprise to anyone. Hopefully the church has already witnessed your service and character and sees this as a natural step. Of course, the size of your church will affect this. If you are a member of a massive church, your service and character may have gone unnoticed.

Typically, after a season of evaluation, the church will act formally to endorse or affirm your call to ministry. This looks different church-to-church. Some may affirm your calling by setting you apart for the ministry generally, others by calling you to a specific ministry position, and others in a hybrid fashion. However it goes, this process typically involves a formal ordination council wherein you will be questioned about theological and spiritual matters by a group of ordained men. It will likely culminate in an ordination or installation service of some kind.

Some churches may choose not to set you apart publicly until you actually begin serving in ministry. In other words, they don't ordain you when you are set apart for ministry but when you actually take up ministerial responsibilities. The argument is that you don't ordain someone to hypothetical ministry, but to actual ministry.

I have a slightly different approach. While I agree that you don't ordain someone to hypothetical ministry, I don't think that requires waiting until one is called to serve a particular church vocationally. I argue that, as part of the evaluation process, we should see not only elder-like character, but elder-like gifting and elder-like service already occurring. Of course, you cannot exercise formal authority in the church until you are placed in that position by the church. But you can be teaching and leading as God has given you opportunity and influence.

In all of this, don't be discouraged if the process is slow. The church is to be scrupulous. The call to ministry is sacred, and the church's affirmation is a sacred stewardship. If the church is quick to ordain, that may be a sign of their shallowness, and it can undermine the confidence their affirmation should give you. A rigorous process led by godly men will be a source of reassurance for you for years to come.

A REASSURING CONFIRMATION

While wrestling with my own call to ministry, seven different men whom I respected, over the course of several months, encouraged me to be praying about the ministry. They sensed God might be calling me, and they encouraged me to be open to His leading. Though I didn't have a well-formed understanding of the call to ministry, their encouragement meant a great deal. It confirmed that I wasn't crazy or overassessing myself in contemplating the ministry.

I think of the reassurance that church affirmation gives like cosigning a loan. When a wealthier party cosigns a loan, they are vouching for the applicant's intent to pay it back. They stand with them and believe in them so much that if the applicant doesn't pay it back, they will. Cosigning a loan is a significant step of trust and confidence. So too is a church's commendation. When a church stands with you, vouches for you, and affirms you, you can look back on that for years to come—especially during the trying seasons of ministry—as helpful reassurance.

Regardless of your context, the relative strength or weakness of the congregation, your age or previous service, the local church is the arbiter—the final human evaluator of your call. Spurgeon was spot on when he argued, "The will of the Lord concerning pastors is made known through the prayerful judgment of his church. It is needful as a proof of your vocation that your preaching should be acceptable to the people of God."[2]

Charles Bridges's *The Christian Ministry* is one of the classic works on pastoral service. Though written nearly two hundred years ago, it is timeless—speaking incisive wisdom to the call to ministry. Let's give Bridges the last word on why and how the church should affirm your call to ministry:

The external call is a commission received from and recognized by the Church, not indeed qualifying the minister, but accrediting him, whom God had internally and suitably qualified. This call communicates therefore only official authority. The internal call is the voice and power of the Holy Spirit, directing the will and the judgment, and conveying personal qualifications. Both calls, however— though essentially distinct in their character and source— are indispensable for the exercise of our commission.[3]

Accredited for the ministry—that's what you are when the church affirms your call. Without the church's affirmation, you are a rogue preacher, an unaccredited minister. The relationship between the would-be minister and the church is essential. It is imperative that he receives the church's support, and, as we'll learn next, that the church, in return, receives his love.

QUESTION #6

DO YOU LOVE
THE PEOPLE OF GOD?

Have you ever known a married couple who confessed they didn't love each other? I have, and trust me, there is nothing more painful. As a husband, I can't imagine waking up every morning beside a woman I didn't love. I pity such a person.

On a couple of occasions, I've had such couples meet with me. Their stories tend to be similar. Life is rote. Their relationship is boring. They are married, but they feel more like individuals sharing a home and splitting the bills. For these people, romance left town long ago. They feel trapped because they understand divorce isn't an option.

I can't imagine the boredom, frustration, and disappointment that type of life must entail, especially for those who, like me, believe that marriage is between one man and one woman *for life*.

This is what one who enters the ministry without a love for the church will feel. In many ways, ministry is like marriage; you sacrifice for, love, and serve the body of Christ. You cannot do this—you will not do this—unless you serve out of a heart of love.

Perhaps you've seen pastors like this. They look for every opportunity to be away from their congregation. They erect barriers between themselves and their church. They view other activities, ministerial or otherwise, as more important and more satisfying than just serving God's people. They seem to view God's people as an interruption to their ministry, when the people are supposed to *be* their ministry.

Imagine giving your life to a task you do not love—or worse, to a people you don't love. Ministry service is glorious, but it can also be uniquely taxing, and only those propelled by a love for Christ and His church survive the long haul.

THE NEW TESTAMENT IS
ALL ABOUT THE CHURCH

It is impossible to read the New Testament without being struck by the centrality of the church. In the Gospels, Jesus dies for His church, charges Christians to expand His church, and promises to build His church. In the book of Acts, the church is birthed at Pentecost and explodes into unstoppable expansion and powerful ministry. The Epistles were all written to congregations or individuals about what the church should believe, how it should function, and how it should be led. When we come to the book of Revelation, we see Christ writing seven letters to seven churches and promising to one day return for His bride, the church. This all speaks to the importance of the church—indeed, of Jesus' love for it. In fact, Christ so identified Himself with the church that He famously challenged Saul on the Damascus Road, "Saul, Saul, why do you persecute *me?*" (Acts 9:5, emphasis mine). Saul's occupation was to persecute the church, but to Christ that was tantamount to persecuting His very self.

So we must right off dispel the notion that you can serve Christ without serving the church, or that you can love Christ without loving the church. Such an argument is harmful, goes directly against the grain of the New Testament, undermines the local church and the call to ministry, and will shipwreck your pursuit of Christ and Christian service. You may not serve it directly as a pastor or minister, but you should plan on serving the church at least indirectly in a ministry supportive of, or supervised by, the church. That is fitting and right because the New Testament defines ministry in the context of the local church. In whatever capacity you minister, to serve faithfully is to serve from a heart of love.

SHEPHERD WITH LOVE

Two passages especially are relevant for considering the shepherd's love for the sheep. I have returned to them often over the years to remind myself how I should approach God's people. Hear Peter's charge to pastors in 1 Peter 5:1–4. Are you willing to lead God's people in this way?

> Therefore, I exhort the elders among you, as your fellow elder and witness of the sufferings of Christ, and a partaker also of the glory that is to be revealed, shepherd the flock of God among you, exercising oversight not under compulsion, but voluntarily, according to the will of God; and not for sordid gain, but with eagerness; nor yet as lording it over those allotted to your charge, but proving to be examples to the flock. And when the Chief Shepherd appears, you will receive the unfading crown of glory.

Pastoral ministry is first and foremost heart work. God gives the pastor sheep to feed, love, protect, and lead. That is why Peter instructs us to shepherd the flock, not drive the herd. The faithful pastor moves gently among the flock, serving them with a hand of compassion, motivated by a heart of love.

If 1 Peter 5:1–4 is a prescriptive charge to pastors, the following is a description of that charge lived out, as seen in Paul's relationship with the church at Thessalonica.

For you yourselves know, brethren, that our coming to you was not in vain, but after we had already suffered and been mistreated in Philippi, as you know, we had the boldness in our God to speak to you the gospel of God amid much opposition. For our exhortation does not come from error or impurity or by way of deceit; but just as we have been approved by God to be entrusted with the gospel, so we speak, not as pleasing men, but God who examines our hearts.

For we never came with flattering speech, as you know, nor with a pretext for greed—God is witness—nor did we seek glory from men, either from you or from others, even though as apostles of Christ we might have asserted our authority. But we proved to be gentle among you, as a nursing mother tenderly cares for her own children. Having so fond an affection for you, we were well-pleased to impart to you not only the gospel of God but also our own lives, because you had become very dear to us.

For you recall, brethren, our labor and hardship, how working night and day so as not to be a burden to any of you, we proclaimed to you the gospel of God. You are witnesses, and so is God, how devoutly and uprightly and blamelessly we behaved toward you believers; just as you know how we were exhorting and encouraging and imploring each one of you as a father would his own children, so that you would walk in a manner worthy of the God who calls you into His own kingdom and glory. (1 Thess. 2:1–12)

Every time I read this passage I am challenged anew in my love for the church. Paul was the great missionary-theologian of the early church. He penned thirteen New Testament letters, planted churches all across Asia Minor, defended the faith, and suffered for the cause of Christ. He never saw a conflict he wasn't willing to engage. He was a lion, a true gospel warrior. Yet his ministry to the Thessalonians was nonetheless marked by humility, compassion, and service. He loved the saints as his own children.

The same kind of love that Martin Luther challenges ministers to have toward their sheep:

> Men who hold the office of the ministry should have the heart of a mother toward the church. Unless your heart toward the sheep is like that of a mother toward her children—a mother who walks through fire to save her children—you will not be fit to be a preacher. Labor, work, unthankfulness, hatred, envy and all kinds of sufferings will meet you in this office. If, then, the mother heart, the great love, is not there to drive the preachers, the sheep will be poorly served.[1]

LOVE GROWS OVER TIME

You may have the impression that you either love the church or you don't, but that is not the case. Your love for God's people isn't static or zero sum; it can grow and deepen over the years as you deepen your relationships with the congregation.

The first church I pastored, Muldraugh Baptist Church, was a blessing to me, my wife, and our growing family from day one. I continually thank God for the joy of getting to pastor those precious people. One thing I observed in those years was that my love grew as I served, overcoming issues and people that had previously frustrated me. One experience especially stands out.

In my first year at the church, as we approached the Easter season, I was concerned over how full the church's calendar was. I was especially reluctant about leading the sunrise service. Frankly, I had a bad attitude about it from the moment I heard of it. My previous churches did not have a sunrise service, so the concept was foreign to me. Our Holy Week calendar was already beyond full. We had our regular Wednesday evening service, a Maundy Thursday service, a Good Friday service, a Saturday morning Easter egg hunt, and a Saturday evening Easter cantata. On Resurrection Sunday we had a churchwide breakfast during the Sunday school hour, a Sunday morning service, an Easter lunch with church members afterward, and then, lastly, our standard Sunday evening service. I'm all for celebrating the resurrection, but—with fear of sounding sacrilegious—this was a bit much.

Not only was the sunrise service agonizingly early—and outside—but it also meant I had to prepare an additional sermon. I suspected that the only people in attendance would be the ultracommitted, who would be at all the other services and events anyhow. It all struck me as "Exhibit A" of an overscheduled church. Though I desperately did not want to do it, I was new at the church and did not want to cause conflict over matters of preference.

I still remember driving up the gravel road to the lake for my first sunrise service. My wife had our infant daughter out in the morning chill, and I was speaking to about thirty people who were, as I suspected, the ultracommitted. I kept it brief, went through the motions, and then dashed back to the church to review my Easter Sunday sermon. A good attitude I did not have.

I wish I could tell you that someone in attendance called me later that week and said the service touched them profoundly and renewed their spirit, and that it became the highlight of their year. But that's not the case. The reality is, no one left changed—no one, that is, but me. In fact, a funny thing happened. Over the next couple of years, I moved from tolerating the Easter sunrise service, to liking it, to loving it. By year three, I actually looked forward to the sunrise service. The church's Holy Week calendar remained crazy full, the sermon preparation was one more item on my to-do list, and all my other concerns remained, so what changed?

In hindsight, what I discovered was that the more I loved God's people, the more I grew to love what they loved. I grew to care about what they cared about. I grew to desire what they desired. They weren't a group of people I worked for; they were a group of people I lived, ministered, and grew with. It wasn't that the sunrise service became more special to me; it's that God's people became more special to me.

If you find yourself struggling to love the church, I would encourage you in two ways, one theological and the other practical. First, theologically, consider afresh Christ's love for the church. He promised to build the church. He died for the church. He is coming back for the church. You want to love what Christ loves, and Christ loves the church.

Practically, and believing God has providentially called you to shepherd your flock, intentionally spend time with them. Get to know them. Hear their stories. Enter into their lives and let them into yours. Understand that people aren't a hindrance to your ministry; they *are* your ministry. As you do, you'll likely find your love for God's people intensifying month by month.

Those who will enjoy the most satisfying and fruitful ministry are those who adopt Richard Baxter's exhortation, "The whole of our ministry must be carried on in the tender love of our people. We must let them see that nothing pleases us but what profits them."[2] You will encounter people who frustrate you, responsibilities that drain you, and expectations that burden you. But in all these things you will find that only love can compel you to serve, sacrifice, and shepherd. Love is absolutely necessary for the man God has called into the ministry. And as we'll see in the next chapter, love for the church is not all a shepherd must have; he must also love those yet outside the church.

QUESTION #7

_____

ARE YOU PASSIONATE
ABOUT THE GOSPEL AND
THE GREAT COMMISSION?

There is no work quite like PhD work. Those who've completed the degree know exactly what I'm talking about. You must set aside five or so years of your life to research and write, ending your labors with a dissertation that makes a unique contribution to your field of study. The PhD is known as a "terminal degree" because it is the highest anyone can earn, but all who've completed one know it can feel terminal in other ways.

Shockingly, the three letters most associated with the Doctor of Philosophy degree are not PhD. They are ABD— "all but dissertation." Half of those who undertake the PhD degree never complete it, with most stalling out during the dissertation phase.[1]

A good friend who'd completed his PhD a few years before me gave me advice that was, in hindsight, absolutely essential. He told me, "Whatever you do, pick a dissertation topic that absolutely captivates you; that will animate you day in and day out until you finish it."

That was excellent advice. It took me six years to complete my PhD. I was serving full-time at Southern Seminary, had served local churches as a pastor and interim pastor, and was a husband and the father of five young children. For several years, most nights of the week I said goodnight to my wife and children around eight o'clock and worked late into the night on my dissertation.

My friend's advice is good for those entering doctoral work, but it is even better for those contemplating ministry. Unless you have a singular, overarching passion that will pull you forward in ministry, it may be best not to pursue it. As Spurgeon said:

> Brethren, if the Lord gives you no zeal for souls, keep to the lapstone or the trowel, but avoid the pulpit ... We must feel that woe is unto us if we preach not the gospel; the word of God must be unto us as a fire in our bones, otherwise, if we undertake the ministry, we shall be unhappy in

it, shall be unable to bear the self-denials incident to it, and shall be of little service to those among whom we minister.[2]

Is Spurgeon justified in such bold claims? Let's look to the Scriptures to find out.

CHRIST'S COMMISSION, PAUL'S PASSION

Church mission statements are important, but every church's mission statement ought to reflect the Church's mission statement: the Great Commission. On five occasions Jesus gave this abiding command, binding on all churches regardless of location, era, or size. In Matthew 28:18–20 He says:

All authority has been given to Me in heaven and on earth. Go therefore and make disciples of all the nations, baptizing them in the name of the Father and the Son and the Holy Spirit, teaching them to observe all that I commanded you; and lo, I am with you always, even to the end of the age.

Christ's command to make disciples is not reserved for pastors. It is a standing order for every believer and church. But as a minister, you will be tasked week in and out to lead the effort. As Paul exhorted Timothy, so he exhorts us: "Do the work of an evangelist" (2 Tim. 4:5).

It's no wonder Paul exhorted Timothy in this way, since evangelism was his driving passion. Set apart from his mother's womb, Paul was "made a minister according to the stewardship from God bestowed on [him]" (Col. 1:25). On this calling he reflects, "If I preach the gospel, I have nothing to boast of, for I am under compulsion; for woe is me if I do not preach the gospel" (1 Cor. 9:16). Paul preached with urgency and gravity, knowing that eternal life and death hung in the balance for his hearers. God's call and his own desire for his hearers to be saved compelled Paul to minister with all his might.

This is key. Fundamentally, if the ministry is viewed through a humanistic lens, then it is easy to sign up and withdraw whenever, depending on the relative whims of the pastor. This is not consistent with the New Testament calling; the preacher preaches not only because he wants to preach, but because he *must* preach. "Woe is me if I do not preach."

Is Paul just waxing eloquent, or did the fire really burn within his bones? A cursory survey of his letters proves the latter. His heart bled for the lost, and it propelled him forward in gospel ministry, in spite of terror and tumult. For example, consider his words to the church at Rome:

> I do not want you to be unaware, brethren, that often I
> have planned to come to you (and have been prevented so
> far) so that I may obtain some fruit among you also, even

as among the rest of the Gentiles. I am under obligation both to Greeks and to barbarians, both to the wise and to the foolish. So, for my part, I am eager to preach the gospel to you also who are in Rome. For I am not ashamed of the gospel, for it is the power of God for salvation to everyone who believes, to the Jew first and also to the Greek. (Rom. 1:13–16)

In this same letter he also discloses his burden for his own countrymen, the Jewish people, most of whom had rejected Christ:

I am telling the truth in Christ, I am not lying, my conscience testifies with me in the Holy Spirit, that I have great sorrow and unceasing grief in my heart. For I could wish that I myself were accursed, separated from Christ for the sake of my brethren, my kinsmen according to the flesh . . . Brethren, my heart's desire and my prayer to God for them is for their salvation . . . (Rom. 9:1–3; 10:1)

What man would wish for his own separation from Christ for the sake of others? A man with unwavering passion for the Great Commission and love for the lost.

DISCERNING YOUR CALL TO MINISTRY

PERSONAL RESPONSIBILITY

Evangelistic urgency isn't reserved for Paul or an elite class of
super-Christian. Every person in ministry is called to the work
of gospel proclamation. In God's divine economy it is His plan
for reaching the world for the glory of His name. Look at Paul's
airtight logic for gospel ministry. Does it resonate with you?

> For the Scripture says, "Whoever believes in Him will not
> be disappointed." For there is no distinction between Jew
> and Greek; for the same Lord is Lord of all, abounding in
> riches for all who call on Him; for "Whoever will call on
> the name of the Lord will be saved."

> How then will they call on Him in whom they have not be-
> lieved? How will they believe in Him whom they have not
> heard? And how will they hear without a preacher? How
> will they preach unless they are sent? Just as it is written,
> "How beautiful are the feet of those who bring good news
> of good things!" (Rom. 10:11–15)

These verses are special to me because they helped clarify my
own call to ministry, and I still serve with them in mind. Some
days they energize me. Other days they rebuke me. Every day
they drive me.

Your evangelistic urgency will ebb and flow due to many factors, including the receptivity of your hearers, your own spiritual vitality, and other personal and contextual variables. But I know of no better gauge for my spiritual and ministry vitality than my passion for the gospel. If I'm lukewarm about the Great Commission, it points to deeper concerns.

GEORGE WHITEFIELD

Perhaps no one in modern church history exhibited more of a love for the Great Commission than George Whitefield. Whitefield is regarded as one of the greatest, if not *the* greatest, preachers of the English language. Whitefield's evangelistic preaching, along with Jonathan Edwards's, ushered in the Great Awakening in America in the 1740s. It is no overstatement to suggest that Whitefield's ministry accounts for much of America's strong Christian heritage.

Over his three-decades-long ministry, Whitefield crossed the Atlantic thirteen times to preach in both England and North America. In America he rode horseback up and down the Atlantic Seaboard, preaching to crowds numbering ten, twenty, thirty, possibly fifty thousand people. When Whitefield preached in New York, Philadelphia, and Boston—the three largest cities in colonial America—his crowds outnumbered those cities' total populations. Benjamin Franklin himself confirmed these staggering and unprecedented numbers.[3]

Whitefield preached multiple times a day, often through opposition, disruption, persecution, and at least one assassination attempt, and he preached a simple message: you must be born again. He traveled horseback from town to town, without reprieve or respite, and against his physician's stern counsel. Whitefield considered the whole world his parish, so he ministered anywhere and everywhere God would enable him. In fact, he once reflected, "God forbid that I should travel with anybody a quarter of an hour without speaking of Christ to them."

What drove Whitefield to such extremes? Why did God use him so extraordinarily? He had zeal for the Great Commission. His passion was like an artesian well—a continual, ever-replenishing reservoir of ministry energy and endurance. Literally, his passion to preach the gospel went with him to the grave. He preached through infirmity and anguish until his body gave way just hours after preaching his final sermon in Newburyport, Massachusetts, where his remains are buried underneath the pulpit in the Old South Church.

To pursue ministry but not have a passion for the gospel and Great Commission is like pursuing medicine but not liking patients. I suppose you can manage along, but you will lack fruitfulness and joy. Most troubling of all, you will hinder God's divine plan for reaching the world for Christ.

Once, early in my ministry, I was in a particular season of challenge. I found myself frustrated with a family in my church and not sleeping well at night over the disruption they were causing the congregation. That same week, I had the privilege of following up with a couple who had visited our church the previous Sunday. The conversation was a divine appointment, one of those unmistakable occasions when God went before me. That evening, during my visit, both the husband and wife gave their lives to Christ. They continue to follow Jesus, faithfully serving their church. I remember driving home that evening, reflecting that the joys of gospel labor far outweigh ministry challenges.

A passion for the gospel and the Great Commission are qualifications for ministry. Ministry work is gospel work, and both are heart work. A love for the lost and a desire to see them come to know Christ will be forward propulsion for your ministry. Don't embark on ministry without a love for the gospel and the Great Commission. A great barometer for whether you have this love is answering our next question: *Are you engaged in fruitful ministry?*

QUESTION #8

ARE YOU ENGAGED IN
FRUITFUL MINISTRY?

As a child, I grew up in a sports-oriented family. My brothers and I weren't musically inclined, nor were we known to stay up late devouring books. Sports were our thing.

As the youngest of three sons, I saw my brothers (six and eight years older) as my heroes—and in many ways I still do. Both of them were standout athletes, especially on the basketball court. As a preteen I eagerly attended my brothers' games, though I personally was ambivalent about sports. I spent most of my summer days building forts in the woods, catching fish, killing imaginary bad guys, and just trolling around our suburban neighborhood enjoying a rather ideal childhood.

As I approached middle school, I grew increasingly aware of my brothers' reputations as star athletes. I would find myself running on the court after their high school and college games, imagining I was them. I increasingly paid attention to their efforts, reading their newspaper clippings and swelling with pride over their accomplishments.

By the time I became a teenager, my interest in basketball intensified, but there was still an on-again, off-again feel to it all. About the time my second brother signed his college scholarship, I really began to sense the pressure to play—and play well.

People asked me daily if I would play basketball like my brothers. I found myself giving a confident "yes," but I never pursued the sport with focus or discipline. It was as though, since everyone else assumed I would play, I did, too. "Why not," I thought. "I have my brothers' height and last name. All is set."

As I approached high school my assumptions were tested. I sensed that my visions of athletic grandeur were ill-founded. I had not put in the practice time, and I was not excelling when I did play. It finally hit me one day when my father laid it out. It's been some twenty-five years, but I remember his words as if he said them yesterday.

He said, "You don't just walk on the court when you are eighteen and decide you want to be a college athlete. It starts *now*. It starts in the driveway, at the gym, in the weight room, and on the court. If you want to be a college athlete later, you must begin living like one now." In other words, the one who will play basketball in college is the one playing—and playing well—as a teen.

I've never forgotten my father's counsel, and I often share it with aspiring ministers. Those who can be most confident about their fitness for ministry are those most actively engaged in ministry now. Are you engaged in fruitful ministry?

EXPERIENTIAL, NOT HYPOTHETICAL

Ministry is not something we undertake after earning a seminary degree or other earthly credential. It is not so much a vocational jump as it is a vocational migration.

This is my story. Before I shared with others my sense that God was calling me to ministry, before I took a vocational ministry position or underwent the ordination process, I began serving my church in ministry-like roles. I taught Bible studies, preached in prisons and halfway houses, and led evangelistic outreach events. One reason I was confident God was calling me to ministry was that I was serving in ministry and enjoying God's favor and pleasure in it.

Consider the lead-up to marriage. On June 26, 1999, I formally committed my life to my wife, Karen, in holy matrimony. I loved that girl and was irresistibly drawn to the altar, eager to spend the rest of my life with her. On that day, before God and gathered witnesses, I publicly promised what had been welling up in my heart for many months. My love for her had already shown itself in a thousand ways; instinctively I bought her flowers, spent time with her, and dreamed of our future together. The wedding ceremony was the final, glorious testimony of what was increasingly settled in my heart. God didn't flip a love-switch in my heart at the moment we were wed. My love for Karen progressed from bud to full bloom in the season leading up to our wedding day. I was ready to state my commitment to Karen because I already *had* committed myself to her in my heart.

Similarly, the person most likely called to ministry is the person already practicing it; and the one who is most likely to know God's blessing is the one already experiencing it. Often, by the time you choose to enter the ministry, you realize you've already chosen it in countless aspirations and forms.

A PASTOR IS KNOWN BY HIS FRUIT

If you read Paul's New Testament letters closely, you will see that he often draws a connection between his ministry calling and his ministry fruitfulness, authenticating the former by evidence of the latter.

To the Corinthians, Paul wrote:

Do we need, as some, letters of commendation to you or from you? You are our letter, written in our hearts, known and read by all men; being manifested that you are a letter of Christ, cared for by us, written not with ink but with the Spirit of the living God, not on tablets of stone but on tablets of human hearts. (2 Cor. 3:1–3)

In the first century, a teacher often used "letters of commendation" to authenticate themselves. We might think of it as a referral letter. Paul points the Corinthians to themselves, and his work among them, as sufficient authentication for his ministry.

Consider also what Paul wrote to the Philippian believers:

I thank my God in all my remembrance of you, always offering prayer with joy in my every prayer for you all, in view of your participation in the gospel from the first day until now. For I am confident of this very thing, that He who began a good work in you will perfect it until the day of Christ Jesus. For it is only right for me to feel this way about you all, because I have you in my heart, since both in my imprisonment and in the defense and confirmation of the gospel, you all are partakers of grace with me. (Phil. 1:3–8)

Paul is confident that his prayer on behalf of the Philippians will be answered because his ministry among them has born increasing fruit. He knows God is blessing the work.

Like he does with other New Testament congregations, Paul reminds the Philippian and Corinthian believers of God's work through him in their lives, with the aim to encourage them and validate his ministry. He references this work not as a point of personal pride, but as a warm reflection on God's call and favor on his ministry and on the church.

Charles Spurgeon, too, sees fruitfulness in ministry as an integral mark of one's call. In *Lectures to My Students*, a classic that belongs on every minister's bookshelf, Spurgeon boldly claims that the authenticity of one's call to ministry is measured by the fruitfulness of his service:

> In order to further prove a man's call, after a little exercise of his gifts, such as I have already spoken of, he must see a measure of conversion work going on under his efforts . . .
>
> It seems to me, that as a man to be set apart to the ministry, his commission is without seals until souls are won by his instrumentality to the knowledge of Jesus. As a worker, he is to work on whether he succeeds or not, but as a minister he cannot be sure of his vocation till results are apparent . . . There must be some conversion-work in your irregular

labours before you can believe that preaching is to be your life-work . . . Prophets whose words are powerless, sowers whose seed all withers, fishers who take no fish, soldiers who give no wounds—are these God's men? Surely it were better to be a mud-raker, or a chimney-sweep, than to stand in the ministry as an utterly barren tree . . .[1]

Spurgeon speaks forcefully here, arguably too forcefully. But the point is worth pondering: to the extent that we see God changing lives through our ministry, we can gain assurance He has indeed set us apart to it. The point is not so much how many lives have been changed, but if lives have been changed.

True, there are times in the Bible when God raises up a prophet to be, in essence, a prophet of doom. The prophet Jeremiah had such a ministry. He was sent as God's agent to deliver words of warning and judgment. But Jeremiahs are the exception, not the rule. Typically, those called to ministry will see—at least to some degree—fruit in their ministry.

What might fruit in ministry look like? There are various forms it might take. It could include people coming to Christ through your influence, Christians being enriched by your biblical teaching, or your church being strengthened in doctrine and ministry vitality through your service.

If you are trying your hand in ministry but God's blessing seems distant, the lost are not being reached, and believers aren't growing from it, it may indicate God is not calling you. It definitely indicates you should give more time to prayer, careful reflection, and the seeking of wise counsel.

In any discussion of fruit in ministry, we must keep in mind that God is the one who grants it (1 Cor. 3:7). Many choice servants, including courageous missionaries, have labored years without seeing converts or growth. In some contexts, fruitfulness looks a lot like faithfulness. The point is not that unless you are seeing fruit in ministry, you aren't called. The point is that as you see fruit in ministry, it can grant you greater assurance that God has indeed called you.

New Student Orientation is one of my favorite days of the academic semester. It happens right before classes begin, and the president's address is my best effort to welcome new students, acclimate them to seminary life, and position them for success as a student—and more importantly, for success in ministry. In those settings I always charge our new students to find a local church and faithfully serve it. I tell them the church needs actual servants, not theoretical ones. I remind them that any church looking to hire a minister wants to know that their candidate has been engaged in ministry, not that they merely intend to be.

My primary goal with those new students is not to better position them for ministerial employment. The same is true for this book; it's not a manual for a job interview. This chapter, this entire book, is intended for something much more important—to help you sort out God's will for your life and to discern if He is calling you to ministry.

Are you already engaging in ministry and seeing the fruit of your labors? That is a good indicator God has set you apart for ministerial service. It is a sign of your commitment to the church, as is your willingness to defend the faith, the next commitment to examine in discerning your call to ministry.

QUESTION #9

ARE YOU READY
TO DEFEND THE FAITH?

I'm a Southerner by birth, and Southerners love a good story. I'm a minister by calling, and I give my life to the preaching and teaching of God's Word and to training others in doing the same. Therefore, for me, a good story is about a great saint heroically defending the faith.

One of the greatest men of church history was Charles Spurgeon, and one of the great stories of church history is his valiant effort to defend the faith, especially as seen through the prism of the Downgrade Controversy. Spurgeon has long been a hero of mine. He's like an old friend who has been good to me, and I want to make sure you are well acquainted with him, too.

THE DOWNGRADE CONTROVERSY

The year was 1887, and Spurgeon was in the winter of his life. For more than three decades he had enjoyed the status of the world's most well-known preacher, but just over the horizon storm clouds gathered.

The Downgrade Controversy began slowly at first, with three anonymous letters appearing in the March, April, and June 1887 editions of the *Sword & Trowel*. The three letters, later revealed to be authored by Spurgeon's friend Robert Shindler, warned of doctrinal slippage on a downhill slope (hence "downgrade").

While the anonymous letters drew interest, the controversy did not explode until a few months later, when Spurgeon directly entered the fray. In the August 1887 issue of the *Sword & Trowel*, he threw down the gauntlet in his six-page editorial titled, "Another Word on the Downgrade."

At that time, Spurgeon was less than five years from his death. He was near the height of his popularity in the Baptist Union and beyond, but near the depth of his personal anguish. Physical ailments like failing kidneys and chronic gout wracked his body; depression plagued his soul. Simply put, he did not need, nor was he much poised for, the conflict he was about to enter. Withdrawing the largest Baptist church in England from the Union would have dire consequences. Nevertheless, Spurgeon entered his Westwood study, took pen in hand, and proceeded to join the battle himself by drafting for publication the six-page article.

I own the original six-page manuscript Spurgeon wrote that day in 1887. It is fascinating to review his words, penned in his own hand, with his markings, alterations, and emphases. It radiates the spirit of Paul and the urgency of keeping the faith. The first paragraph especially has taken on immortality:

No lover of the gospel can conceal from himself the fact that the days are evil. We are willing to make a large discount from our apprehensions on the score of natural timidity, the caution of age, and the weakness produced by pain; but yet our solemn conviction is that things are much worse in many churches than they seem to be, and are rapidly trending downward. Read those newspapers which represent the Broad School of Dissent, and ask yourself, How much farther could they go? What doctrine remains to be abandoned? What other truth to be the object of contempt? A new religion has been initiated, which is no more Christianity than chalk is cheese; and this religion, being destitute of moral honesty, palms itself off as the old faith with slight improvements, and on this plea usurps pulpits which were erected for gospel preaching. The Atonement is scouted, the inspiration of Scripture is derided, the Holy Spirit is degraded into an influence, the punishment of sin is turned into fiction, and the resurrection into a myth, and yet these enemies of our faith expect us to call them brethren, and maintain a confederacy with them![1]

Most prophetically, Spurgeon argued that true believers cannot be ministry affiliates with those who have compromised the faith. His words portended the schism to come. Spurgeon was a lone voice, but he was the loudest and most revered voice of all, calling for doctrinal fidelity over programmatic confederation.

Spurgeon's "Another Word on the Downgrade" landed like a bombshell. It sent shockwaves throughout the Baptist Union and British evangelicalism. It reverberated throughout the Protestant world.

For decades the press had attacked Spurgeon, but now he would be savaged by his own Baptist Union. Prior to the Downgrade Controversy, if the Baptist Union had a papacy, Spurgeon would've been the unquestioned pope, but now his former brethren brutalized him. They charged him with pugilism (fighting) and being a schismatic. They even questioned his sanity with a whisper campaign that his physical ailments had rendered him mad. Graduates of Spurgeon's College turned on him, and the leaders of the Baptist Union scorned him.

Over the next two months, Spurgeon penned two more articles on the Downgrade in the *Sword & Trowel*. Then, on October 28, 1887, Spurgeon wrote the General Secretary of the Baptist Union, Samuel Harris Booth, to announce his withdrawal from the Baptist Union.

Three months later, in January 1888, the Baptist Union Council voted to accept his withdrawal, and then the council of nearly a hundred members voted to censure Spurgeon, with only a meager five men supporting the Prince of Preachers.

The Baptist Union adopted a *compromise* doctrinal statement, which was altogether too weak—neither clear nor comprehensive enough. Though now outside the Union, Spurgeon still opposed the statement for its obvious deficiencies. Nonetheless, it passed overwhelmingly, by a vote of two thousand to seven, and could be appropriately interpreted as a second vote against Spurgeon. Most tragically, Spurgeon's brother, James, seconded the motion to pass the statement.

The controversy cost Spurgeon dearly. It cost him friendships. It cost him his reputation. Even his own brother disowned his decision. Yet, for Spurgeon, to remain within the Union would be tantamount to theological treason.

Spurgeon kept the faith, and this must be our aspiration—to keep the faith even when confronted with our own Downgrade

Controversies. Spurgeon's story brings us to our next question: *Are you ready to defend the faith?*

DEFENDING THE FAITH, A TIMELESS CHARGE

As we've seen throughout this book, a call to the ministry is a call to the ministry of the Word. As such, we are called not only to proclaim it but also to defend it. The New Testament Epistles overflow with injunctions to guard the truth. Reflect on Paul's words to Timothy—a mere sampling of the New Testament charges to defend the faith—and let their import for you and your call to ministry sink in:

- "As I urged you . . . instruct certain men not to teach strange doctrines" (1 Tim. 1:3).
- "Retain the standard of sound words" (2 Tim. 1:13).
- The church is "the pillar and support of the truth" (1 Tim. 3:15).
- "Be diligent to present yourself approved to God as a workman who does not need to be ashamed, accurately handling the word of truth" (2 Tim. 2:15).
- The Lord's servant is to gently correct those who "are in opposition, if perhaps God may grant them repentance leading to the knowledge of the truth" (2 Tim. 2:25).
- "You followed my teaching, conduct, purpose, faith,

patience, love, perseverance, persecutions, and sufferings . . ." (2 Tim. 3:10–11a).

- "Continue in the things you have learned and become convinced of" (2 Tim. 3:14).
- "Preach the word; be ready in season and out of season; reprove, rebuke, exhort, with great patience and instruction. For the time will come when they will not endure sound doctrine; but wanting to have their ears tickled, they will accumulate for themselves teachers in accordance to their own desires, and will turn away their ears from the truth and will turn aside to myths. But you, be sober in all things, endure hardship, do the work of an evangelist, fulfill your ministry" (2 Tim. 4:2–5).
- "I have kept the faith" (2 Tim. 4:7).

Paul speaks through Timothy to us, his charges echoing through the ages. As Christian ministers, we must be ready and willing to defend the faith. If ministers don't do it, who will? That is one reason why God placed the "able to teach" qualification in 1 Timothy 3.

The concern is not eloquence but the ability to rightly study, interpret, teach, and apply God's Word. The truth is the bone marrow of the church. When the truth is compromised, the church withers. Vibrant mission and ministry do not occur where there is doctrinal decay.

And as you go about the business of defending the truth, be encouraged, God will defend you. As you care for the truth, God will care for you. As A. W. Tozer once said, "God will never let a man starve to death for telling the truth—remember that, my friend."[2]

DEFENDING THE FAITH, A TIMELY CHARGE

While every generation is called to defend the faith, our generation especially is called to this responsibility. The twenty-first century is the age of apostasy. Theological liberalism has fully metastasized globally. In its wake are shipwrecked ministers, undermined faith, dead churches, and dying denominations. In addition to theological liberalism, we are also confronted by social and cultural upheaval. All of this makes the twenty-first century a uniquely challenging and exhilarating time to minister.

With the sexual revolution now having come full bloom, and the American public having largely accepted same-sex marriage, pressure for the church to fold on issues of sexuality, gender, and marriage will only intensify. Orthodoxy has never been popular, and it will be decreasingly so.

There is an unavoidable collision of worldviews, and the irony is that the more our culture tries to silence us, the more the minister must speak, because the church must be strengthened and warned. Now is the time for the strongest men to preach the strongest sermons in the context of the strongest churches. You don't need to be a trained apologist. Though God gifts His church with such persons, that may not necessarily be your calling. You must, however, in your own context and with your own abilities, be ready and willing to study and speak the truths of Scripture.

At its most basic level, to prepare to defend the faith—in the words of Peter—is to "sanctify Christ as Lord in your hearts, always being ready to make a defense to everyone who asks you to give an account for the hope that is in you" (1 Peter 3:15).

You can't defend the faith without having studied it. First, you must study the faith so you don't inadvertently fall into error yourself. Heresy is unwittingly preached in evangelical churches every Sunday by ill-equipped pastors. That's a tragedy, and you don't want to be among their number. You don't have be an honors student, just a diligent one. After all, as a general rule, God has chosen not to populate the ranks of his ministers with the wise or the noble, but with those who are willing to be counted a fool for His sake.

More broadly, you must study the truth so you can uphold and pass on biblical, orthodox Christianity. As you study, you'll find how well the Bible defends itself. As Spurgeon once quipped, "Defend the Bible? I would as soon defend a lion! Unchain it and it will defend itself."[3]

Spurgeon died less than five years after the Downgrade Controversy. Against his previously stated wishes, his supporters erected a massive marble burial tomb in the West Norwood Cemetery in London. Inscribed on the front in an opened Bible is 2 Timothy 4:7, "I have fought a good fight, I have finished my course, I have *kept the faith*."

Spurgeon died having kept the faith, and we should have the same aspiration. Ministers are called to share their faith, but they are also called to keep it. Are you ready and willing for the task? It will certainly cost you, and this leads us to our last question: *Are you willing to surrender?*

QUESTION #10

ARE YOU WILLING
TO SURRENDER?

Ageneration ago, "surrendering to ministry" was a common phrase in evangelical churches. It was certainly common in my childhood church. Most every sermon ended with an invitation to surrender to ministry. This immediately followed our pastor's appeal to follow Christ, be baptized, or join the church.

As a boy, the phrase "surrender to ministry" both mystified and unnerved me. It sounded as though one was embracing an unwanted life, a call to a distant land for an undesired work. It seemed like a call one intuitively resisted—as long as possible —until finally buckling under the Spirit's pressure and embarking on a life of ministry that, albeit noble, would be marked by sacrifice and hardship.

In hindsight, I do not think that is what my pastor meant, nor do I think that is what the New Testament implies. As I found in my own life, surrendering to ministry is not caving to an unwanted vocation; it is embracing what becomes increasingly irresistible: gospel ministry.

In other words, if by surrendering to ministry we mean engaging in an undesirable work, then jettison that phrase now. But if we mean surrendering to minister as unto the Lord and self-consciously choosing to forgo other life opportunities, conveniences, and ambitions, then surrendering to ministry is a good, healthy phrase. In fact, I am convinced "surrendering to ministry" is a phrase the church needs to recover and a ministry-posture the church needs to cultivate. Every faithful ministry begins with a surrendered life, and that submissiveness shapes every aspect of one's ministry, including why, where, and what one preaches. This leads us to our final question: *Are you willing to surrender?*

WHAT SURRENDER ENTAILS

Surrendering to ministry rightly establishes the pastor's motivation. After all, the pastor's incentive should not be material gain, the applause of men, or any other earthly enticement.

Rather, the preacher should, like the apostle Paul, know in his heart, "If I preach the gospel, I have nothing to boast of, for I am under compulsion; for woe is me if I do not preach the gospel" (1 Cor. 9:16).

To surrender to preach the ministry is to be so gripped by God's call, and so moved for His glory, that one shares Jeremiah's burden: "If I say, 'I will not remember Him or speak anymore in His name,' then in my heart it becomes like a burning fire shut up in my bones; and I am weary of holding it in, and I cannot endure it" (Jer. 20:9).

The urgency with which one preaches may ebb and flow based on a multitude of factors, including the receptivity of the congregation, the preacher's spiritual vitality, and the tenor of the text itself. But, for the man rightly surrendered to ministry, the "why" of the ministry is settled—it is for Christ and His glory.

Additionally, surrendering to ministry includes a determination to follow God's call *wherever* it may lead. This may include a willingness to leave family and friends, go to a distant place, and undertake a new work. After all, Jesus reflected, "Foxes have holes, and the birds of the air have nests, but the Son of Man has nowhere to lay his head" (Matt. 8:20). Too many ministers are perfectly willing to follow God's call as long as it does not lead out of their hometown. Such kingdom restrictiveness is alien to the New Testament and stymies one's availability to be used by God. Practically speaking, you can know if you are limiting God's call if you've already placed—perhaps even unconsciously—limits on where you are willing to serve Christ.

A willingness to go wherever includes a willingness to minister to *whomever*. There are churches across the land poised for anything but numerical success. Challenging demographics, an unreceptive audience, or a dilapidated neighborhood might make God's call unattractive, but if it is God's call, it is a glorious one—regardless of the zip code. After all, struggling churches and dying communities need ministers, too. God typically calls more to a people than a place. If God calls you to minister to a church in a challenging area, are you willing to go?

Surrendering to ministry also means operating under the authority of God's Word. Most especially, this relates to the act of preaching itself. The role of the preacher is not to cobble together anecdotes with human insights and then sprinkle in a couple of Bible verses to produce a "homily." The faithful preacher tunes his ear to the Spirit of God, not the critic's grumble. His finger is on the text, not in the air, gauging the wind. His voice is given to preaching the Word, not peddling shallow sermons for shallow people.

Too many pastors are textual acrobats, contorting their preaching to avoid Scripture's sharper edges. Such preachers have become adept at explaining away difficult texts and dodging confrontational verses. From the earliest days of ministry you'll have to guard your heart from pleasing anyone other than the Lord. Fearing combative personalities, overreacting to legitimate criticism, or stubbornly desiring man's approval can all compromise your message and disorient you from your paramount loyalty: loyalty to the One who called you—God Himself.

TWO STORIES OF SURRENDER

The Bible offers no better case study of surrendering to ministry than the Old Testament prophet Jonah. God called Jonah to go to Ninevah and preach repentance so the people there might be saved. It's crystal clear that God was concerned about the why, where, and what of Jonah's message.

Tragically, Jonah resisted God's call in spectacular fashion. When God called Jonah, he was in Israel. God instructed him to go to Ninevah, which was about 550 miles east of Jerusalem in what is now modern-day Iraq, but Jonah did the exact opposite. He struck out for Tarshish, located in modern-day Spain, some 2,000 miles in the opposite direction!

Why did Jonah resist God's call to preach repentance to the Ninevites? The Ninevites were the sworn enemies of the Israelites. The last thing Jonah wanted was to see the Ninevites repent and escape God's impending judgment. In fact, Jonah actually confessed that he fled to Tarshish because he knew God was "gracious and compassionate, slow to anger and abundant in lovingkindness, and one who relents concerning calamity" (Jonah 4:2).

God's ministers are not spiritual free agents. We are not ecclesiastical entrepreneurs who strike out on our own and minister in accordance with our own desires. As Jonah's sin was running *from* God's appointed place of ministry, a more common twenty-first-century sin might be running *to* a preferred place of ministry.

On the contrary, aspire to be like John Piper, who went to Bethlehem Baptist Church in 1980 despite a small, aging congregation in dilapidated facilities located in a transitional neighborhood. He sensed God's call, followed it, and has been used by God like few others in our generation.

A number of years ago I faced a similarly challenging decision. A church reached out to me about helping them through a season of challenge and transition. I felt God's leading to serve the church, but several friends sought to dissuade me. I vividly recall one friend telling me, "Stay away. That church will ruin your resume. It's a troubled congregation in a troubled part of town. Billy Graham couldn't grow that church. You'll have plenty of great opportunities in the years ahead. Don't settle for anything less than God's best for you."

Though well intended, that counsel was altogether unhelpful and disorienting. For a while it confused me, until I remembered that God's will for my life *is* God's best for my life. By enlarging my circle of wise counselors, reflecting on the church's needs, and my wife and I seeking the Lord and gaining His peace, it became clear that God was indeed calling us to that church.

The bottom line is, if you had a million lives to live you could not improve upon the life God has called you to live and the ministry to which He has called you. Don't settle for second best by choosing the path of least resistance or the ministry that promises the best payout. Seek God's will and surrender to it.

At this point, your sense of calling is probably far more opaque and generic than Jonah's. That's perfectly fine. The point is not that you must be certain of the specific ministry God is calling you to undertake. The point is that you don't enter ministry with your fingers crossed. You don't hedge your bets. You certainly don't plan on negotiating your "terms of surrender" with God. God negotiates with no one, including you.

These days the phrase "surrendering to ministry" seems a vestige of the previous generation of church life. This is more than unfortunate; it is unhealthy, and the church is the big loser.

Surrendering to ministry means you're willing to go to anyone, anywhere, anytime. But don't be confused; as you surrender you will enter more fully into God's joy and blessing. A surrendered life is integral to a healthy ministry.

CONCLUSION

SO ARE YOU CALLED?

Have you ever received a physical, a thorough examination of your body to evaluate your health? A few years ago, for reasons that remain unclear to me, my wife began insisting that I receive a thorough physical examination. Being the sensitive and responsive husband that I am, I steadfastly resisted her suggestion. Nothing about volunteering for a physical examination appealed to me.

I thought I had sufficiently put the issue to bed, then several months later I came down with a sinus infection. This was routine for me. I typically come down with a sinus infection a couple of times a year. When I do, I just zip by our family physician, get a couple of prescriptions, and am quickly on my way.

But this time was different. As I sat in the small room waiting for the doctor to enter, I noticed what struck me as unnecessary equipment. The room must have been preset for the next patient, I thought.

When the doctor entered the room, I discovered that my wife had not forgotten about the physical, and had covertly arranged for me to have just that. And a thorough physical examination I did receive. I was poked, probed, and prodded. I was relentlessly interrogated. I left as one having been thoroughly examined. My routine doctor's appointment turned out to be anything but routine.

Though I had steadfastly resisted such a comprehensive physical evaluation, I was reassured when all of my test results came back. I had been given a clean bill of health.

As we come to the end of this book, perhaps you feel a bit like I did at the doctor's office. You have subjected yourself to a thorough spiritual examination. You have been inundated with questions. Your doctrinal beliefs and ministry qualifications have been probed; your assumptions, emotions, and passions have been prodded. Your calling has been scrutinized.

Having undergone this evaluation, where do you now stand? Are you called to ministry? Are you confident God has set you apart to be His servant and spokesperson, and are you ready to pursue His call on your life?

Let's review our ten questions. Let them probe your heart one final time:

1. Do you desire the ministry?
2. Does your character meet God's expectations?
3. Is your household in order?
4. Has God gifted you to preach and teach His Word?
5. Does your church affirm your calling?
6. Do you love the people of God?
7. Are you passionate about the gospel and the Great Commission?
8. Are you engaged in fruitful ministry?
9. Are you ready to defend the faith?
10. Are you willing to surrender?

Can you affirmatively answer these ten questions?

I CAN . . . WHAT SHOULD I DO NEXT?

If this *is* you, and you have gained confidence God has called you to ministry, you may be awash in emotions. You are likely humbled by God's call and eager to pursue it, yet uncertain and perhaps even fearful about what your first steps should be.

Without question, you should seek out your pastor and pursue his affirmation and counsel, as well as that of your entire church and its leadership. As we've seen throughout this book, meeting the qualifications of 1 Timothy 3 and receiving the affirmation of God's people are essential. Once these matters are certain, you should pursue ministry preparation with all that you have.

If you've gained clarity and assurance that God has, in fact, set you apart for ministry, I want to point you forward for maximum kingdom impact. Before putting this book down, take time to reflect with me on why you should pursue ministry preparation and how to optimize it.

Why you should pursue ministry preparation

The call to ministry is a call to prepare, and ministry preparation is as old as the church itself. The apostle Paul received personal instruction from Christ, and he exhorted Timothy to "Be diligent to present yourself approved to God as a workman who does not need to be ashamed, accurately handling the word of truth" (2 Tim. 2:15). Paul's exhortation to Timothy rings through the ages, challenging every generation of gospel ministers to be maximally prepared for ministerial service.

A ministerial amateur is *not* one who lacks formal training or advanced degrees from reputable institutions. An amateur is one who lacks the knowledge base, skill set, and experience for a particular task—in this case, Christian ministry. This means that one can still be an amateur though holding an earned degree, and one can be a faithful minister though lacking one.

In fact, Christians, and especially ministers, are called to be 1 Corinthians 1 people, confidently preaching the foolishness of the cross. Moreover, the list of those who lacked formal theological training while impacting the world for Christ is long, including luminaries such as John Bunyan, Charles Spurgeon, and Martyn Lloyd-Jones. I have learned much from men who lacked formal education.

Yet, never before in the history of the church has theological education been so accessible, and never before has it been so needed. Advanced technology, innovative delivery systems, and proliferating resources all make being a ministerial amateur as a permanent state inexcusable.

The complexity of our times

Our culture necessitates rigorous ministry preparation. Every generation presents the church with particular challenges, but our generation comes with unique baggage. It is not that the twenty-first century is more fallen or more secular than previous ones, but it may be more complex. There are befuddling ethical questions, often tortuously complex ramifications of sin, and a cultural intelligentsia devoting its best energies to undermining the Christian belief system. All these present the church with serious challenges. The lost need more than shallow answers from ill-equipped ministers. They need ministers prepared to bring the full complement of Christian truth to bear in a winsome, thoughtful, and compelling way.

The centrality of teaching the Scriptures

The preaching and teaching of Holy Scripture is the principal responsibility of the Christian minister, and it is the central need of the church. Paul repeatedly charged Timothy to a faithful ministry of the Word with exhortations like, "retain the standard of sound words" (2 Tim. 1:13), "guard . . . treasure the truth which has been entrusted to you" (1:14), "accurately handle the word of truth" (2:15), and "preach the Word" (4:2). These exhortations, and many others, require a renewed and informed mind. There is simply no place in ministry for sloppy exegesis, shoddy interpretation, or shallow sermons. One can be a faithful minister without a seminary degree, but one cannot be a faithful minister without knowing the Bible well.

The consequences of ministry

There is an alarming inverse correlation between the seriousness of the ministerial task and the casualness with which it is often approached. We would not let an untrained mechanic rebuild our transmission or permit an unlearned pediatrician to diagnose our children. Yet churches often place individuals with the lowest levels of preparation in the highest office.

Why would one knowingly receive soul care and biblical

instruction from an amateur? And why would a minister be content as one? Souls hang in the balance. There is a heaven to gain and hell to shun. There is fixed truth to defend and proclaim. Satan is serious about his calling; ministers must be serious about theirs. The ministry is too consequential to be taken casually.

The priority of the Great Commission

The end to which the minister labors is the proclamation of the gospel and the furtherance of the Great Commission. Fulfilling the Great Commission necessitates a burden for the lost, a passion for the glory of God in the salvation of sinners, *and* an equipped mind to reason, teach, and persuasively present the gospel. Though often thought of primarily as an act of zeal, the Great Commission also requires knowledge. It requires a readiness to "give an account for the hope that is in you," an ability to "contend earnestly for the faith which was once for all handed down to the saints," and the skill to teach these things "to faithful men who will be able to teach others also" (1 Peter 3:15; Jude 1:3; 2 Tim. 2:2).

I CAN'T . . . WHAT SHOULD I DO NEXT?

If you find yourself not confident that God has set you apart, it could be due to a number of reasons.

First, it may be that God is, in fact, not calling you to ministry. Knowing that is a good thing. You are not a second-class Christian; rather you are, in God's will, not pursuing ministry. You can still glorify Christ in your nonministerial vocation, and you should resolve to do just that. Nearly every semester I'll have a student who leaves seminary having concluded God has not called them to full-time ministry. If a person leaves seminary due to sin, lack of self-discipline, or some other regrettable circumstance, that is always a sad occasion. But if a person leaves seminary simply because they've clarified and confirmed God is leading them in a different direction with their lives, that is a good thing.

Second, maybe you aren't settled on God's call because you could not satisfactorily answer one or more of these ten questions. Perhaps you are still growing in the spiritual disciplines, settling your theological convictions, or yet to find opportunities to serve your church. In these scenarios, it may not be a permanent "no," but a temporary one. Continue to seek God's will, continue to interatct with these ten questions, and continue to look for open doors for ministry, trusting that in God's timing He'll open them.

Third, you may not have clear, objective reasons why you shouldn't pursue ministry at this time. Perhaps you just have a general unease, a lack of confidence, a nagging self-doubt. That does not necessarily mean you shouldn't pursue ministry.

Once again, I'd point you to your pastor and elders. They can help you search your heart and sense God's leadership. In any healthy church, your leadership will love you enough to point you in the right direction.

In summary, in all that you do, resolve to follow God's call on your life. As you do, you'll know His favor and His joy, and you'll be positioned to glorify Him, in ministry or not.

APPENDIX

ADVICE FOR SEMINARY

As you've sensed throughout this book, I'm passionate about the ministry and about training those who are called to it, so I want to offer you a few parting words of encouragement on ministry preparation, particularly about seminary. Obviously I'm a tad biased toward the institution I lead—Midwestern Baptist Theological Seminary—but there are a number of healthy, commendable evangelical seminaries in North America, and my goal isn't to persuade you to attend any certain one. It is to make sure you pick a quality seminary and get the most out of it while you're there.

Choose your seminary wisely

From the outset, one's choice of a seminary is crucial. Is the institution you have selected doctrinally faithful? Does it serve the local church and love the Great Commission? Is its faculty willing to invest in you personally? These questions and more are worth carefully pondering. If any of these issues are awry, transfer immediately. You only attend seminary once; do not settle for a subpar institution.

Thankfully, there are many healthy seminaries in North America. But for every healthy one there are many that are unhealthy, so you must choose wisely. Paul exhorted Timothy, "Pay close attention to yourself and to your teaching; persevere in these things, for as you do this you will ensure salvation both for yourself and for those who hear you" (1 Tim. 4:16). A great seminary spends the bulk of its energy helping you fulfill this charge. As you do, you will have laid the foundation for a faithful ministry, one that saves you and those who sit under you.

Consider an MDiv

In the world of theological education, the Master of Divinity degree (MDiv) has long been the gold standard for ministry preparation, and its status is well deserved. In it one finds the complete tool kit for preparing for ministry service: Greek and Hebrew, New Testament and Old Testament studies, and classes in theology, church history, preaching, pastoral care and counseling, evangelism, missions, and more.

The priority of the MDiv degree is not rooted in what it offers, but in what ministers and churches need. Ours is an exhilarating age to live in and minister. The unpredictable challenges of a decadent culture, the perennial needs of the church, and the demands of twenty-first century Christian service all point to the urgency and relevance of the MDiv. In other words, the needs of the church are great, and the church's expectations of their ministers will be greater still.

While the sad reality is that many church members have a lack of biblical knowledge, that is no permission slip for ministers to exhibit the same. God doesn't grade ministers on the curve. We are judged by New Testament standards, not by whether or not we know the Scriptures marginally better than ill-informed church members. All whom God has called must be ready to serve Him. Don't settle for the quickest or easiest degree; instead aim for being as prepared for a lifetime of faithful ministry as you can be. Completing an MDiv does not ensure a faithful ministry, but it does best position one for it. If at all possible, don't settle for anything less.

Get the most out of seminary

While in seminary, you quite literally are spending a few years (and not a little money) to prepare for several decades of ministry. Get the most out of it. Assuming you have been prudent in selecting a seminary, drink deeply from the well while you are there. Attend chapel services and special events. Build relationships with your faculty. Intentionally seek out mentors. Be prepared for class. You only enjoy the opportunity once; don't waste it.

Cultivate habits that will sustain a lifetime of ministry

Seminary can be a challenging season. Many students hold down multiple jobs, parent a growing family, and live with the constant pressures of classroom assignments. For some students, this crucible is unlike anything they have encountered before. To manage it well, self-discipline, careful stewardship of time, and the ability to prioritize the best over the good are indispensable habits to form. If you cultivate these habits in seminary, they will serve you well for the rest of your ministry. Get creative with managing your schedule and guarding study time.

Build relationships

To this day, many of my closest friends in ministry are men I met at seminary. The challenge of rigorous study, the joy of those romantic early years in ministry, and similar life stages, are the perfect setting to build ministry relationships that last. My wife also forged some of her closest relationships during those years. For us, these relationships have been a constant source of encouragement as we have traveled the highs and lows of life and ministry.

Be about the basics

The longer I serve in ministry, the more I realize how important the basics of Christian discipleship truly are. The purpose of theological education is to enhance and extend the basics of the Christian life, not eclipse them. For the seminarian, it is all the more urgent to read your Bible daily, study it regularly, pray often, share Christ *at least* once a week, cultivate personal holiness, and practice other spiritual disciplines. Jesus found the lukewarm church nauseating. How much worse is the lukewarm minister?

Serve your local church

The church is not a place you go to work in ministry after graduation. The church *is* your ministry, then and now. Join a healthy church and find a way to serve it during seminary. This will beautifully complement and balance your studies. It will also help you when you seek your first vocational ministry position. As I said earlier, churches want to hire proven ministry servants, not hypothetical ones. Show yourself faithful to God's people before you are on their payroll.

Think practically about the theological

Roughly speaking, seminary classes will range from the theological to the practical. Some classes, like theology, apologetics, and church history, are more content-driven. Do not leave them there. Seek to apply what you learn to your life and ministry. Think through ways you can teach theology to your congregants. Imagine how apologetics informs your personal evangelism. Realize that church history is more than names and dates, and instead draw practical encouragement from the great cloud of witnesses God has used throughout the church's history.

Think theologically about the practical

Similarly, the practicalities of ministry ought to have a biblical and theological foundation. Preaching, administering the ordinances, conducting funerals and marriages, rightly ordering the church, applying leadership principles, and every other practical dimension of ministry should be—and must be—informed biblically and theologically. A good professor will connect the dots, but make sure you connect them as well. The practical is always theological, and vice versa.

Do not lose your family while gaining a degree

Last, but certainly not least, guard your family. The old axiom is true, "It is better get an 'A' at home and a 'C' in the classroom than an 'A' in the classroom and a 'C' at home." One should strive to get an "A" in both realms, but if something has to give, do not let it be your family. You can have a great marriage without a great ministry, but you can't have a great ministry without a great marriage.

I once heard a professor rebuke a student who argued it was appropriate to read his sermon manuscripts because Jonathan Edwards read his. The professor shot back, "You fool, you're no Jonathan Edwards." Similarly, don't look to models like Spurgeon and Lloyd-Jones as justification for not pursuing formal theological education. They were self-taught geniuses. Likely, you are not. God may well use you in spite of a lack of formal training, but if you can access a theological education— and virtually every person on the planet now can—why find out? Ministers will be judged for their faithfulness, not their academic accomplishments, but it is impossible to be faithful without being rightly equipped. Brother, do not be an amateur minister.

NOTES

Introduction: *What Does It Mean to Be Called to Ministry?*

1. John Newton, *The Works of John Newton* (Carisle, PA: Banner of Truth, 2015), 62.
2. Often attributed to Martin Luther, source unknown.
3. Oswald Chambers, from *My Utmost for His Highest* in *The Complete Works of Oswald Chambers* (Grand Rapids: Discovery House, 2013), 828.

Question #1: *Do You Desire the Ministry?*

1. Iain Murray, *D. Martyn Lloyd-Jones: The First Forty Years, 1899–1939* (Edinburgh: Banner of Truth, 1982), 80.
2. Martyn Lloyd-Jones, *Preaching and Preachers* (Grand Rapids: Zondervan, 1972), 105.
3. Alexander Strauch, *Biblical Eldership: An Urgent Call to Restore Biblical Church Leadership* (Colorado Springs: Lewis and Roth, 1995), 281.
4. J. E. C. Welldon, "The Difficulty of Preaching Sermons," in *The Living Age,* seventh series, vol. 25 (Oct.–Dec. 1904), 267.
5. C. H. Spurgeon, *Lectures to My Students* (Peabody, MA: Hendrickson, 2010), 26.

Question #2: *Does Your Character Meet God's Expectations?*

1. Taken from the article "Extending the Gift of Welcome to All" in the fall 2012 edition of *Mosaic*, the institutional publication of Louisville Presbyterian Theological Seminary.
2. A useful resource for more interaction with this subject is *Women in the Church: An Analysis and Application of 1 Timothy 2:9–15* by Andreas J. Köstenberger and Thomas R. Schreiner (Baker Academic).
3. Taken from a transcript of John MacArthur's sermon "The Qualifications for a Pastor, Part 2: Noble Character, Part 2," on December 13, 1992.

4. A. W. Tozer, "Sheep Are Led," *Tozer for the Christian Leader: A 365-Day Devotional,* compiled by Ron Eggert (Chicago: Moody, 2015), March 14 entry.

Question #4: *Has God Gifted You to Preach and Teach His Word?*

1. C. H. Spurgeon, *Autobiography, Volume 1: The Early Years* (London: Banner of Truth, 1962), v.
2. Lloyd-Jones, *Preaching and Preachers*, 9.

Question #5: *Does Your Church Affirm Your Calling?*

1. Lloyd-Jones, *Preaching and Preachers*, 114.
2. C. H. Spurgeon, *Lectures to My Students*, 29.
3. Charles Bridges, *The Christian Ministry* (Carisle, PA: Banner of Truth, 1958), 91–92.

Question #6: *Do You Love the People of God?*

1. Martin Luther, "Ministers," in *What Luther Says: A Practical In-Home Anthology for the Active Christian*, ed. Ewald M. Plass (1959: repr., Saint Louis: Concordia, 1994), 932.
2. Richard Baxter, quoted in *Preacher and Pastor*, ed. Edwards A. Park (Andover: Allen, Morrill, and Wardell, 1845), 325.

Question #7: *Are You Passionate about the Gospel and the Great Commission?*

1. Laura Morrison, "Why Do People Drop Out of Ph.D. Programs?", GradSchools.com, April 2014, http://www.gradschools.com/get-in-formed/surviving-graduate-school/life-during-graduate-school/why-do-people-drop-out-phd.
2. C. H. Spurgeon, *Lectures to My Students*, 26–29.
3. Thomas Kidd, *George Whitefield: America's Spiritual Founding Father* (New Haven, CT: Yale University Press, 2014), 84–85.

Question #8: *Are You Engaged in Fruitful Ministry?*

1. C. H. Spurgeon, *Lectures to My Students*, 29.

Question #9: *Are You Ready to Defend the Faith?*

1. Charles Spurgeon, "Another Word on the Downgrade," *The Sword and the Trowel*, August 1887.
2. A. W. Tozer, address on WMBI Saturday Morning Radio, "Talks from a Pastor's Study" segment (Chicago, March 7, 1959).

3. This is a paraphrase of a larger quotation from an address Spurgeon
   gave to the Bible Society in 1875. Variations occur in at least two of his
   Metropolitan Tabernacle sermons (Nos. 2004 and 2467).

ACKNOWLEDGMENTS

Most every writing project, including a sole-authored book, is actually a collaborative effort. As I wrap up *Discerning Your Call to Ministry*, I feel this reality more than ever. I am grateful to so many who have given so much for this project to come to completion. First, my wife, Karen, and our five children have been a constant source of encouragement. They are a vast reservoir of love, joy, and energy, always rooting for me in every ministry endeavor, including this book.

My office staff, including Patrick Hudson, Dawn Philbrick, Catherine Renfro, and Jake Rainwater, have all provided encouragement and technical support. They are a steady source of support and a delight to serve with. Additionally, colleagues such as Jason Duesing and Owen Strachan kindly read over the manuscript. For their encouragement and input I remain grateful.

Finally, I am truly grateful for the team at Moody Publishers, who saw fit to publish this project, and, more broadly, to partner with Midwestern Seminary in the "For The Church" imprint. The entire team, including Adam Dalton, Randall Payleitner, Matthew Boffey, and Parker Hathaway, have been a delight to partner with on this project.

Most of all, I am grateful to my Lord and Savior, Jesus Christ. He saved me, changed me, and called me to the ministry. May this book, and all that I do, bring Him much glory and honor.

FROM ONE PASTOR
TO ANOTHER . . .

In *On Pastoring*, H. B. Charles gives 30 instructive reflections on the pastor's heart, leadership, and public ministry, covering topics like:

- Cultivating personal godliness
- Prioritizing your family
- Guarding your ministry effectiveness
- Planning, preparing, and preaching sermons
- Balancing pastoral roles and duties

Being a pastor means wearing many hats, weathering pressure, and bearing great responsibility. Let H. B. Charles be a trusted advisor as you do the serious work of shepherding a flock of God.

ALSO AVAILABLE AS AN EBOOK

FOR THE **CHURCH**

MOODY
Publishers®

RADICAL

WITH DAVID PLATT

Radical with David Platt, a half-hour national teaching program, airs daily on Moody Radio. Bestselling author, sought-after conference speaker, and pastor, David Platt brings to each program solid, passionate Bible teaching aimed at equipping and mobilizing Christians to make disciples among the nations so that the Lord receives the glory due His name.

www.radicalwithdavidplatt.org

MOODY
Radio™

From the Word to Life